Shallot Sensations: 94 Delicious Recipes

Heavenly Hot Dips Yash

Contents

3

INTRODUCTION

Shallot Sensations: 94 Delicious Recipes - A Culinary Journey

Cookbooks are a treasure trove of recipes that are both tasty and nourishing. They offer recipes that are easy to follow, ingredients that are readily available, and techniques that are well tested. A cookbook is something that you can rely on when you want to impress your guests or cook a delicious meal for yourself and your family.

Shallot Sensations is no exception. It is a cookbook that is filled with 94 delicious recipes that will delight your taste buds and leave you satisfied. The cookbook is centered around the humble shallot, a vegetable that is often overlooked but adds a unique flavor and texture to any dish. This cookbook is a culinary journey that will take you around the world and introduce you to a variety of cultures through their cuisine.

The author of Shallot Sensations, Jane Washington, is a well-known chef who specializes in creating recipes that are both delicious and nutritious. Her passion for cooking started at an early age, and she has since honed her skills over the years. Jane believes that cooking is an art form, and she loves experimenting with different ingredients to create new and exciting dishes.

In Shallot Sensations, Jane brings together her love for cooking and her expertise to create a cookbook that showcases the shallot in all its glory. The recipes in this cookbook are divided into chapters based on the type of meal, making it easy to find a recipe for any occasion. From breakfast to dinner, appetizers to desserts, this cookbook has it all.

The recipes in Shallot Sensations range from simple and easy to prepare to more complex dishes that require a bit more time and effort. The cookbook contains recipes that are suitable for both beginners and experienced cooks, ensuring that everyone can find something to suit their taste buds. Jane has included detailed instructions for each recipe, making it easy to follow and recreate the dish at home.

One of the standout features of Shallot Sensations is the variety of cuisines represented in the cookbook. Jane has included recipes from around the world, including French, Italian, Indian, Thai, and Mexican cuisine. This makes the cookbook a great resource for those who want to explore new flavors and cuisines.

Not only are the recipes delicious, but they are also healthy. Jane is a firm believer in using fresh and healthy ingredients in her cooking, and she has applied this philosophy to all the recipes in this cookbook. She has included nutritional information for each recipe, making it easy for readers to make informed decisions about their food choices.

Overall, Shallot Sensations is a fantastic cookbook that is perfect for anyone who loves to cook and experiment with new ingredients. The cookbook is packed with delicious, healthy, and easy-to-follow recipes that are sure to impress your family and friends. The next time you want to try something new in the kitchen, grab a copy of Shallot Sensations, and embark on a culinary journey that will take you around the world!

1. Shallot vinaigrette

Shallot Vinaigrette is a simple and delicious dressing perfect for topping a wide variety of salads.
Serving: 4
Preparation Time: 10 minutes
Ready Time: 10 minutes

Ingredients:
• 2 tablespoons white wine vinegar
• 2 tablespoons chopped shallots
• 2 tablespoons extra-virgin olive oil
• 1 tablespoon Dijon mustard
• Salt and fresh ground pepper, to taste

Instructions:
1. In a medium bowl, whisk together the vinegar, shallots, olive oil and mustard.
2. Season with salt and pepper.
3. Serve over your favorite salad.

Nutrition Information (per serving/1 tablespoon):
• Calories: 60
• Total Fat: 6 g
• Cholesterol: 0 mg
• Sodium: 60 mg
• Total Carbohydrate: 2 g
• Dietary Fiber: 0 g
• Protein: 0 g

2. Shallot and garlic bread

Shallot and Garlic Bread
Serving: 4
Preparation Time: 10 minutes
Ready Time: 25 minutes

Ingredients:
- 4 TBSP unsalted butter
- 4 cloves garlic, minced
- 2 large shallots, thinly sliced
- ½ tsp dried thyme
- 4 slices sourdough bread
- ½ cup freshly grated Parmesan
- 1 TBSP freshly-chopped parsley

Instructions:
1. Preheat oven to 350°F.
2. In a small saucepan, melt butter over medium heat.
3. Add garlic and shallots and cook until lightly golden, about 5 minutes.
4. Add thyme and cook for another 2 minutes.
5. Arrange bread slices on a baking sheet.
6. Brush melted butter mixture over each slice.
7. Sprinkle Parmesan over each slice.
8. Bake for 15 minutes, or until lightly golden brown.
9. Garnish with parsley.

Nutrition Information: Serving size = 1 slice, Calories = 234, Total Fat = 11 g, Saturated Fat = 7g, Sodium = 334 mg, Total Carbohydrates = 24 g, Dietary Fiber = 1g, Protein = 8g.

3. Shallot and herb butter

Shallot and Herb Butter is an easy to make recipe bursting with flavour. Perfect for spreading over meats, vegetables or even bread, it can be stored for up to one week.
Serving: Makes about 12 tablespoons
Preparation Time: 5 minutes
Ready Time: 5 minutes

Ingredients:
- 1 shallot, finely chopped
- 8 tablespoons of butter (softened to room temprature)
- 1 tablespoon of fresh thyme
- 1 teaspoon of parsley

- 1 tablespoon of chives
- 2 cloves of garlic, finely chopped
- Pinch of salt and black pepper

Instructions:
1. In a bowl, combine butter, shallot, thyme, parsley, chives, garlic, salt and pepper. Stir until all Ingredients are combined.
2. Using a rubber spatula or wooden spoon, spread the butter onto a sheet of parchment paper. Roll into a log shape and set aside to chill in the fridge for at least 1 hour.
3. Once chilled, cut off desired amount of butter and use as desired.

Nutrition Information:
Calories: 70 Kcal, Total Fat: 7.5 g, Sodium: 37 mg, Carbohydrates: 0.2 g, Protein: 0.2 g

4. Shallot and goat cheese tart

Shallot and goat cheese tart

Serving: 4
Preparation time: 15 minutes
Ready time: 35 minutes

Ingredients:
• 2 oz of refrigerated, store-bought puff pastry, thawed according to package Instructions
• 2 eggs
• 1/4 cup heavy whipping cream
• 8 tablespoons of grated goat cheese
• 1 shallot, finely chopped
• 2 teaspoons of fresh thyme leaves
• 1/4 teaspoon salt
• 1/4 teaspoon black pepper

Instructions:
1. Preheat the oven to 375 degrees F.

2. On a lightly floured surface, roll out the puff pastry into a 10-inch round. Place the pastry on a lightly greased baking sheet.
3. In a small bowl, whisk the eggs and cream together.
4. Spread the goat cheese over the pastry, leaving a one-inch border.
5. Sprinkle with chopped shallot, thyme leaves, salt, and pepper.
6. Pour the egg mixture over everything.
7. Bake for 25 to 30 minutes, until golden brown.
8. Let cool for 5 minutes before slicing.

Nutrition Information:
Calories: 300, Fat: 20 g, Saturated fat: 8 g, Cholesterol: 80 mg, Sodium: 210 mg, Carbohydrates: 19 g, Protein: 8 g

5. Shallot and Parmesan crisps

Shallot and Parmesan Crisps - the perfect combination of sharp and tangy, this recipe is sure to provide an extra crunch to any meal.
Serving: Makes about 40 crisps
Preparation Time: 10 minutes
Ready Time: 20 minutes

Ingredients:
• 2 tablespoons of extra-virgin olive oil
• 2 shallots, peeled and thinly sliced
• 1/2 cup freshly grated Parmesan cheese
• 1/2 teaspoon freshly ground black pepper
• 1/4 teaspoon of sea salt

Instructions:
1. Preheat the oven to 375 degrees Fahrenheit.
2. In a large bowl, stir together the extra-virgin olive oil, shallots, Parmesan cheese, black pepper and salt until the Ingredients are completely blended.
3. Drop the cheesy shallot mixture by the teaspoonful onto a parchment-lined baking sheet, leaving about 1 to 2 inches between each scoop.
4. Bake for 15 to 20 minutes, or until the shallot and Parmesan crisps are golden brown and crispy.
5. Remove from the oven and let cool before serving.

Nutrition Information:
One serving of Shallot and Parmesan Crisps contains approximately 35 calories, 2.37g of fat, 2.1g of carbohydrates, and 1.25g of protein.

6. Shallot and tomato tart

Shallot and Tomato Tart: A delicious tart made from shallots and tomatoes that is sure to tantalize the taste buds!
Serving: 4
Preparation Time: 25 minutes
Ready Time: 50 minutes

Ingredients:
- 3 shallots, thinly sliced
- 2 tablespoons olive oil
- 1 baking sheet, lightly greased
- 1 sheet frozen puff pastry, thawed
- 2 tomatoes, thinly sliced
- 2 tablespoons chopped fresh basil
- Salt and pepper to taste

Instructions:
1. Preheat oven to 350°F.
2. Heat olive oil in a skillet over medium heat. Add shallots and cook until softened and slightly golden.
3. Place puff pastry on greased baking sheet. Arrange tomato slices in a single layer on top of pastry, followed by a layer of shallots. Sprinkle top with chopped basil, salt, and pepper.
4. Bake in preheated oven for 25–30 minutes, or until crust is golden brown.

Nutrition Information:
Calories: 188Kcal; Carbohydrates: 13g; Protein: 2.6g; Fat: 13.7g; Saturated Fat: 3.5g; Sodium: 141mg; Potassium: 176mg; Fiber: 1.3g; Sugar: 2.0g; Vitamin A 4035IU; Vitamin C: 21mg; Calcium: 13mg; Iron: 1.2mg

Shallot and thyme roasted chicken is an easy and delicious recipe that combines the rich flavor of shallots and fragrant thyme to impart a flavor-filled meal.
Serving: This recipe serves 4 people.
Preparation Time: 10 minutes
Ready Time: 1 hour

Ingredients:
- 4 skin-on, bone-in chicken thighs
- 2 tablespoons olive oil
- 4 shallots, peeled and sliced
- 2 teaspoons thyme leaves
- 2 cloves garlic, minced
- 2 teaspoons salt
- 2 teaspoons black pepper

Instructions:
1. Preheat oven to 375 degrees.
2. Place the chicken thighs in a large oven-safe baking dish.
3. In a bowl, mix together the olive oil, shallots, thyme leaves, garlic, salt, and pepper and spread over the chicken.
4. Roast the chicken in the preheated oven for about 30 minutes.
5. Increase the oven temperature to 400 degrees and continue to roast for another 30 minutes or until the chicken is fully cooked and golden brown.
6. Let the chicken rest before serving.

Nutrition Information:
Servings: 4; Calories: 205kcal, Total Fat: 13.2g, Cholesterol: 49mg, Sodium: 902mg, Total Carbohydrates: 4.1g, Protein: 16.2g.

8. Shallot and mushroom tart

Shallot and Mushroom Tart is a delicious savory dish that is easy to make and perfect for any special occasion. Serve this tart as an appetizer or main course.

Serving: 6
Preparation Time: 25 mins
Ready Time: 50 mins

Ingredients:
- 12 frozen tartlet shells
- 2/3 cup heavy cream
- 1 shallot, finely chopped
- 1 garlic glove, minced
- 4 tablespoon olive oil
- 2 tablespoons fresh thyme leaves
- 2 cups lightly packed mushrooms, sliced
- 1/4 cup grated Parmesan cheese

Instructions:
1. Preheat your oven to 375°F and place the frozen tartlet shells onto a baking sheet.
2. In a medium skillet, heat the olive oil over a medium-high heat. Add the shallot and garlic and sauté for about 5 minutes, stirring occasionally.
3. Add in the mushrooms and thyme, and cook until the mushrooms are tender and lightly browned, about 5 more minutes.
4. Divide the mushroom mixture among the tartlet shells and top each with a tablespoon of the heavy cream. Sprinkle Parmesan cheese over the top.
5. Bake for 25 minutes, until the shells are golden-brown and the cheese is melted and bubbly.

Nutrition Information:
Per Serving (1 tartlet):
Calories: 197, Fat: 12g, Saturated fat: 5g, Carbohydrates: 12g, Sugar: 0.7g, Sodium: 34mg, Protein: 5g

9. Shallot and garlic mashed potatoes

Shallot and garlic mashed potatoes are a flavorful take on the classic side dish that make for a delicious accompaniment to grilled meat or fish.
Serving: 4-6
Preparation Time: 30 minutes
Ready Time: 1 hour

Ingredients:
- 8 medium potatoes
- 2 shallots, finely chopped
- 4 cloves garlic, minced
- 3 tablespoons butter
- 2 cups milk
- Salt and pepper, to taste

Instructions:
1. Peel and cube potatoes, and place in a large pot with enough water to cover. Bring to a boil and cook for 15 minutes, or until potatoes are fork-tender.
2. Meanwhile, melt butter over medium heat in a skillet, and sauté shallots and garlic until tender, about 4-5 minutes.
3. Drain potatoes and return to the pot. Mash potatoes with a potato masher, and then stir in milk, butter and shallot-garlic mixture.
4. Season with salt and pepper, to taste. Serve warm.

Nutrition Information: Calories – 210; Fat – 8.5g; Saturated Fat – 4.5g; Cholesterol – 20mg; Sodium – 240mg; Carbohydrates – 29g; Fiber – 5g; Sugar – 3g; Protein – 6g

10. Shallot and lemon roasted asparagus

This simple yet flavorful side dish is sure to please with its savory combination of roasted shallots and lemon over crunchy asparagus.
Serving: 4
Preparation time: 5 minutes
Ready time: 15 minutes

Ingredients:
• 1 lb asparagus, ends trimmed

- 1 shallot, peeled and very thinly sliced
- Juice from 1 lemon
- 2 tablespoons olive oil
- 2 cloves garlic, minced
- Sea salt and freshly ground black pepper, to taste

Instructions:
1. Preheat oven to 400°F.
2. Place the asparagus on a parchment lined baking sheet.
3. Top with shallots, garlic, and olive oil.
4. Drizzle lemon juice over asparagus.
5. Season with salt and pepper, to taste.
6. Roast for 10-15 minutes, or until asparagus is cooked through and lightly browned.
7. Serve immediately and enjoy!

Nutrition Information: 244 calories, 15g fat, 17g carbs, 4g protein

11. Shallot and bacon quiche

- Shallot and bacon quiche is a delicious and savory dish, made with the combination of shallots, bacon, eggs, cream and cheese. Perfect for brunch or as part of a potluck meal, this quiche is a sure crowd pleaser!
Serving- Serves 6
Preparation Time- 20 minutes
Ready Time- 50 minutes

Ingredients:
- 6 ounces bacon, diced
- 1/2 cup shallots, diced
- 2 cloves garlic, minced
- 8 ounces Gruyere cheese, diced
- 1/2 cup heavy cream
- 4 large eggs
- 1 unbaked 9-inch pastry shell

Instructions:-
1. Preheat oven to 375 degrees F.

2. Cook bacon over medium heat until crispy. Transfer bacon to a bowl and set aside.

3. Add shallots and garlic to the pan and cook until tender, about 4 minutes.

4. In a separate bowl, whisk together the cream, eggs and Gruyere cheese.

5. Place the unbaked pastry shell in a baking dish and pour the cheese mixture over the pastry shell.

6. Sprinkle the bacon and shallots over the cheese mixture.

7. Bake for 35-40 minutes, or until the center is set.

8. Let cool for 10 minutes before serving.

Nutrition Information-
Calories: 289 | Carbohydrates: 9g | Protein: 10g | Fat: 22g | Saturated Fat: 8g | Cholesterol: 135mg | Sodium: 331mg | Potassium: 173mg | Fiber: 0g | Sugar: 1g | Vitamin A: 430IU | Vitamin C: 1.4mg | Calcium: 183mg | Iron: 0.9mg

12. Shallot and herb roasted potatoes

This dish is a delicious side dish perfect for any occasion, containing a savory combination of roasted shallots and herbs with buttery potatoes.
Serving: Serves 4
Preparation time: 10 minutes
Ready time: 40 minutes

Ingredients:
- 2 lbs Yukon Gold potatoes, quartered
- 2 shallots, sliced
- 2 tbsp olive oil
- 2 cloves garlic, minced
- 2 tsp dried rosemary
- 2 tsp dried thyme
- Salt and freshly ground black pepper, to taste
- 2 tbsp chopped fresh parsley

Instructions:
1. Preheat oven to 375 degrees F.

2. In a large bowl, combine potatoes, shallots, oil, garlic, rosemary, thyme, salt and pepper. Toss until potatoes are evenly coated.
3. Place potatoes in a single layer onto a parchment paper-lined baking sheet.
4. Bake for 25-30 minutes, flipping once halfway through, or until potatoes are golden and crispy.
5. Sprinkle with parsley and serve warm.

Nutrition Information: Calories: 213; Fat: 8g; Saturated Fat: 1g; Cholesterol: 0mg; Sodium: 63mg; Carbohydrates: 32g; Fiber: 3g; Sugar: 2g; Protein: 3g.

13. Shallot and goat cheese quiche

Shallot and Goat Cheese Quiche is an easy-to-make dish, perfect for any special occasion or weekday meal. It combines savory shallots with creamy goat cheese and is baked in a buttery pastry shell. This dish is sure to be a hit with family and friends.
Serving: 8
Preparation Time: 20 minutes
Ready Time: 1 hour

Ingredients:
• 1 Piecrust
• 1 tbsp olive oil
• 1 small shallot, finely minced
• ½ cup fresh goat cheese
• ¼ cup Parmesan cheese
• ⅔ cup heavy cream
• ½ tsp Dijon mustard
• 4 eggs
• Pinch of nutmeg
• Salt and pepper, to taste

Instructions:
1. Preheat oven to 375°F (190°C).
2. Place piecrust in a 9-inch round pie pan.

3. Heat the olive oil in a small skillet over medium heat. Add the shallot and cook until just starting to brown, about 3 minutes. Set aside to cool.
4. In a large bowl, combine the goat cheese, Parmesan cheese, heavy cream, and Dijon mustard.
5. Beat the eggs in a separate bowl and then add to the cheese mixture. Stir in the cooled shallots and season with nutmeg, salt, and pepper.
6. Pour the filling into the prepared piecrust and bake in the oven for 25-30 minutes. Let the quiche cool before serving.

Nutrition Information:
Calories: 300; Fat: 22g; Protein: 11g; Carbohydrate: 15g; Cholesterol: 128mg; Sodium: 277mg; Fiber: 1g; Sugar: 1g

14. Shallot and red wine sauce

Shallot and red wine sauce is a rich and flavorful sauce that can be paired with many different dishes. It's a great addition to steak, pork, poultry, and vegetables.
Serving: Serves 4-6
Preparation Time: 10 mins
Ready Time: 20 mins

Ingredients:
• 2 tablespoons olive oil
• 2 shallots, minced
• 2 cloves garlic, minced
• 1 cup red wine
• 1/4 cup low-sodium chicken broth
• 2 teaspoons packed dark brown sugar
• 1/4 teaspoon ground pepper
• 1 tablespoon butter

Instructions:
1. Heat the oil in a medium skillet over medium heat.
2. Add the shallots and garlic and cook, stirring, until softened, about 5 minutes.
3. Add the wine, broth, sugar, and pepper and bring to a boil, stirring to dissolve the sugar.

4. Reduce the heat to medium-low and simmer for 10 minutes.

5.Stir in the butter and simmer for a few minutes longer, stirring frequently, until the sauce is thickened.

Nutrition Information: Per serving: 85 calories; 5g fat; 8g carbohydrates; 1g protein; 55mg sodium.

15. Shallot and garlic roasted vegetables

Enjoy a delicious, aromatic plate of Shallot and Garlic Roasted Vegetables, perfect for a nutritious and filling side dish.
Serving: 4
Preparation Time: 10 minutes
Ready Time: 40 minutes

Ingredients:
•2 medium shallots, chopped
•2 cloves garlic, chopped
•2 bell peppers, sliced
•1 red onion, chopped
•1 zucchini, sliced
•2 tablespoons olive oil
•1 teaspoon salt
•Ground pepper, to taste

Instructions:
1. Preheat oven to 400°F.
2. In a bowl, combine the shallots, garlic, bell peppers, red onion, and zucchini.
3. Drizzle the olive oil over the vegetables and add salt and pepper. Mix until vegetables are evenly coated.
4. Transfer the vegetables to a roasting pan or baking sheet.
5. Roast in oven for 30-40 minutes, stirring occasionally, until vegetables are golden and tender.

Nutrition Information: (Per Serving)
•Calories: 88 kcal
•Fat: 6.6 g

•Carbs: 7.6 g
•Protein: 1.4 g

16. Shallot and Parmesan risotto

This flavorful Shallot and Parmesan Risotto is simply delicious. With a few Ingredients and your favorite stock, you'll have a stunning and flavorful risotto that's sure to please any palate!
Serving: 4
Preparation time: 15 minutes
Ready time: 25 minutes

Ingredients:
- 4 tablespoons extra-virgin olive oil
- 2 shallots, chopped
- 2 cloves garlic, minced
- 1 cup Arborio rice
- 2 quarts vegetable stock
- 1/2 cup freshly grated Parmesan cheese
- Salt and pepper to taste

Instructions:
1. Heat the olive oil in a medium-sized saucepan over medium heat.
2. Add shallots and garlic to the pan and cook for 2 minutes.
3. Add the Arborio rice and stir to combine.
4. Slowly add the vegetable stock, stirring constantly.
5. Bring the mixture to a boil, then reduce the heat to low and simmer for 15 minutes, stirring occasionally.
6. Once the rice is cooked through, remove from heat and stir in the Parmesan cheese.
7. Season to taste with salt and pepper.

Nutrition Information:
Calories: 175; Fat: 9g; Carbs: 17g; Protein: 5g; Fiber: 1g; Sugar: 0g; Sodium: 118mg

17. Shallot and herb roasted salmon

This shallot and herb roasted salmon recipe is simply delicious. The combination of freshly chopped herbs, shallots, and lemon adds deliciousness to the salmon. Serve with your favorite side dish and you have a restaurant-quality meal in under 30 minutes.
Serving: 4
Preparation Time: 10 minutes
Ready Time: 20 minutes

Ingredients:
- 1 1/2 lbs. salmon fillet
- 2 large shallots, finely chopped
- 2 tbsp. olive oil
- 2 tbsp. fresh herbs of your choice (e.g. dill, parsley, chives)
- 2 cloves garlic, minced
- Juice of 1 lemon
- Salt and pepper to taste

Instructions:
1. Preheat oven to 350°F.
2. Line a baking sheet with parchment paper.
3. Place salmon fillet on the parchment paper.
4. In a small bowl mix together shallots, olive oil, herbs, garlic, lemon juice, salt and pepper.
5. Spread the shallot mixture over the top of the salmon fillet.
6. Bake in the preheated oven for 15-20 minutes or until salmon is cooked through.
7. Serve with your favorite side and enjoy!

Nutrition Information: 195 Calories; 12g fat; 1g Carbohydrates; 22g Protein

18. Shallot and mushroom risotto

Creamy and delicious, this Shallot and Mushroom Risotto is a great Italian meal that everyone will love.
Serving: 4-6

Preparation Time: 25 minutes
Ready Time: About 1 hour

Ingredients:
- 2 shallots, diced
- 2 tablespoons olive oil
- 4 cups vegetable or chicken broth
- 8 ounces cremini mushrooms, sliced
- 1 1/2 cups arborio rice
- 1/4 cup dry white wine
- 2 tablespoons butter
- 1/2 cup freshly grated Parmesan cheese
- 2 tablespoons fresh chives, chopped, for garnish

Instructions:
1. Heat a medium-sized saucepan over medium heat and add the olive oil and diced shallots. Cook for 4-5 minutes until shallots are softened.
2. Add the mushrooms and cook for an additional 3-5 minutes until lightly browned.
3. Increase the heat to high and add the broth and rice. Cook for 15-20 minutes, stirring occasionally, until most of the broth is absorbed and the rice is cooked through.
4. Reduce the heat to low and stir in the wine and butter.
5. Stir in the Parmesan cheese and cook for an additional 3-5 minutes until the cheese is melted and the risotto is creamy.
6. Serve in bowls and garnish with fresh chives. Enjoy!

Nutrition Information: per serving (142g): Calories 308, Fat 7.1g, Saturated Fat 2.5g, Protein 8.1g, Carbohydrates 46.7g, Fiber 1.6g, Sugar 1.9g, Sodium 280mg

19. Shallot and garlic roasted pork loin

This classic dish of Shallot and Garlic Roasted Pork Loin will definitely make a great meal. It's a simple dish, seasoned with shallots, garlic, and herbs, and roasted to juicy perfection.
Serving: 4 servings
Preparation Time: 5 minutes

Ready Time: 1 hour 10 minutes

Ingredients:
- 1 2-3 lb pork loin
- 4 large shallots- finely chopped
- 3 cloves garlic- finely chopped
- 2 tablespoons olive oil
- 1 teaspoon dried thyme
- 1 teaspoon dried rosemary
- 2 teaspoons salt
- 1 teaspoon pepper

Instructions:
1. Preheat oven to 350 degrees F (175 degrees C).
2. Rinse pork loin and pat dry. Place in a roasting pan.
3. In a small bowl, combine the shallots, garlic, olive oil, thyme, rosemary, salt, and pepper. Rub the mixture all over the pork loin.
4. Roast in preheated oven for 1 hour, or until internal temperature reaches 145-155 degrees F (63-68 degrees C).

Nutrition Information:
Per Serving: 303 calories; 11.5 g fat; 19.4 g carbohydrates; 33.7 g protein; 77 mg cholesterol; 627 mg sodium.

20. Shallot and feta cheese salad

This Shallot and Feta cheese salad is a perfect mix of crunchy, savory, and zesty flavors! This simple and refreshing salad is perfect for a light summer meal.
Serving: 4
Preparation Time: 10 minutes
Ready Time: 10 minutes

Ingredients:
- 2 shallots, finely diced
- 6 tablespoons crumbled feta cheese
- 2 tablespoons extra-virgin olive oil
- Juice of one lemon

- Kosher salt and freshly ground pepper, to taste

Instructions:
1. In a medium bowl, combine the shallots, feta cheese, olive oil, and lemon juice.
2. Season with salt and pepper to taste, and stir to combine.
3. Serve chilled or at room temperature.

Nutrition Information (per serving):Calories: 140, Total Fat: 12g, Saturated Fat: 3.5g, Polyunsaturated Fat: 1.5g, Monounsaturated Fat: 8g, Sodium: 334mg, Potassium: 65mg, Carbohydrates: 7g, Sugar: 2g, Protein: 2g, Vitamin A: 1.2%, Vitamin C: 4.6%, Calcium: 9.2%, Iron: 1.6%

21. Shallot and herb roasted beef tenderloin

This roasted Shallot and Herb beef tenderloin is a savory and delicious main dish. With a combination of seasonings and herbs, this beef dish is perfect for entertaining or Sunday dinner.
Serving: Serves 8
Preparation Time: 15 minutes
Ready Time: 1 hour

Ingredients:
• 2-pound beef tenderloin
• 2 tablespoons olive oil
• 2 tablespoons freshly chopped parsley
• 2 large cloves garlic, minced
• 2 Shallots, peeled and minced
• 1 teaspoon dried oregano
• 1 teaspoon dried basil
• 1 teaspoon dried rosemary
• Salt and pepper to taste

Instructions:
1. Preheat the oven to 375°F.
2. Place the beef tenderloin in the center of a roasting pan.

3. In a small bowl, mix together the olive oil, parsley, garlic, shallots, oregano, basil, rosemary, salt, and pepper.
4. Rub the mixture all over the beef tenderloin.
5. Place the roast in the preheated oven and bake for 45 minutes.
6. Remove the roast from the oven and let it rest for 10 minutes before slicing.

Nutrition Information:
Calories (per serving): 252; Fat (g): 13; Carbohydrates (g): 1; Protein (g): 27; Sodium (mg): 37.

22. Shallot and goat cheese salad

Shallot and Goat Cheese Salad is a flavorful easy to make salad packed with rich and creamy Ingredients. It's perfect for a light lunch or as a side salad for dinner.
Serving: 6
Preparation Time: 10 minutes
Ready Time: 10 minutes

Ingredients:
• 4 ounces soft goat cheese
• 2 tablespoons olive oil
• 1 shallot, thinly sliced
• 2 teaspoons honey
• 2 tablespoons chopped fresh mint leaves
• 4 small heads of radicchio lettuce
• Sea salt and freshly ground black pepper, to taste

Instructions:
1. In a medium bowl, combine the goat cheese, olive oil, shallot, honey, and mint. Mix until fully blended.
2. Separate the radicchio leaves and divide them among six plates.
3. Divide the goat cheese mixture among the plates, spooning it generously over the radicchio leaves.
4. Sprinkle with sea salt and freshly ground black pepper.
5. Serve and enjoy.

Nutrition Information:
- Calories: 142
- Total Fat: 8g
- Saturated Fat: 3g
- Cholesterol: 8mg
- Sodium: 102mg
- Total Carbohydrate: 11g
- Dietary Fiber: 3g
- Protein: 6g

23. Shallot and lemon grilled shrimp

Shallot and lemon grilled shrimp is an easy and delicious seafood dish that's perfect for a light lunch or dinner. With the combination of sweet and savory flavors, it's sure to be a hit!
Serving: 8 servings
Preparation time: 10 minutes
Ready time: 25 minutes

Ingredients:
-3 tablespoons olive oil
-1 tablespoon freshly squeezed lemon juice
-2 teaspoons minced garlic
-2 teaspoons minced fresh herbs, such as thyme, oregano, and parsley
-2 shallots, thinly sliced
-1/2 teaspoon ground black pepper
-2 pounds medium shrimp, peeled and deveined

Instructions:
1. Preheat a grill to medium-high heat.
2. In a small bowl, mix olive oil, lemon juice, garlic, herbs, shallots, and pepper.
3. Coat the shrimp in the citrus-shallot mixture.
4. Place the shrimp onto the pre-heated grill and cook for about 5 minutes per side, or until the shrimp is pink and cooked through.
5. Serve hot.

Nutrition Information (per serving):

Calories: 149 kcal, Carbohydrates: 2 g, Protein: 24 g, Fat: 6 g, Saturated Fat: 1 g, Cholesterol: 165 mg, Sodium: 257 mg, Potassium: 165 mg, Fiber: 1g, Sugar: 1g, Vitamin A: 98 IU, Vitamin C: 7 mg, Calcium: 92 mg, Iron: 2 mg

24. Shallot and bacon potato salad

This delicious Shallot and Bacon Potato Salad is the perfect way to add some flavor to your lunch or dinner. It's a combination of roasted potatoes, shallots, bacon, and a creamy dressing that comes together in no time!
Serving: 4
Preparation Time: 10 minutes
Ready Time: 30 minutes

Ingredients:
• 4 to 5 Yukon potatoes, diced and roasted
• 2 tablespoons olive oil
• 2 large shallots, sliced
• 120g bacon, cooked and diced
• 2/3 cup mayonnaise
• 1 tablespoon white wine vinegar
• 2 tablespoons fresh chives, chopped
• Salt and pepper, to taste

Instructions:
1. Preheat oven to 375°F.
2. Place diced Yukon potatoes on a baking tray lined with parchment paper. Drizzle with olive oil, salt and pepper and toss to coat. Roast in oven for 20 minutes.
3. In a large bowl, combine the roasted potatoes, shallots, bacon, mayonnaise, white wine vinegar and chives. Mix until well combined.
4. Let cool for 10 minutes before serving. Enjoy!

Nutrition Information:
Serving size: 1/4

Calories: 237kcal | Fat: 16.4g | Saturated Fat: 3.6g | Cholesterol: 13mg | Sodium: 298mg | Carbohydrates: 17.4g | Fiber: 2.6g | Sugar: 2.3g | Protein: 8.3g

25. Shallot and herb roasted root vegetables

Shallot and Herb Roasted Root Vegetables is an easy and nutritious side dish. This recipe serves 4 and takes 30 minutes to prepare and 40 minutes to cook.

Ingredients:
- 2 large potatoes, peeled and cubed
- 2 large sweet potatoes, peeled and cubed
- 2 large carrots, peeled and sliced into rounds
- 2 large parsnips, peeled and cubed
- 1 large shallot, finely chopped
- 2 TBSP olive oil
- 1 TBSP dried oregano
- 1 TBSP dried thyme
- 1 tsp garlic powder
- Salt and pepper to taste

Instructions:
1. Preheat oven to 375°F
2. In a large bowl, combine potatoes, sweet potatoes, carrots, parsnips, and shallot.
3. Drizzle olive oil over the vegetables and toss until evenly coated.
4. Add oregano, thyme, garlic powder, salt, and pepper. Toss to combine.
5. Spread vegetables in a single layer on a parchment paper-lined baking sheet.
6. Bake for 40 minutes or until vegetables are cooked through and beginning to crisp.

Nutrition Information (per serving):
Calories: 270 kcal
Fat: 8g
Carbohydrates: 47g
Protein: 5g

Sugar: 7g
Sodium: 135mg
Fiber: 9g

26. Shallot and Parmesan roasted Brussels sprouts

This Shallot and Parmesan Roasted Brussels Sprouts recipe is a quick way to prepare flavorful Brussels sprouts! The Parmesan cheese gives the vegetable an extra cheesy and nutty flavor that pairs perfectly with the caramelized shallots.
Serving: 6
Preparation Time: 15 minutes
Ready Time: 30 minutes

Ingredients:
-1.5 lbs Brussels sprouts, halved
-3 shallots, thinly sliced
-3 tbsp olive oil
-1/3 cup Parmesan cheese, grated
-Salt and pepper to taste

Instructions:
1. Preheat the oven to 400 degrees Fahrenheit.
2. Place halved Brussels sprouts on a baking sheet, and spread out shallot slices in between.
3. Drizzle the olive oil over the vegetables, and then season with salt and pepper.
4. Cook in preheated oven for 20 minutes.
5. Sprinkle Parmesan cheese over the Brussels sprouts, and cook for an additional 10 minutes, or until desired crispness is achieved.

Nutrition Information: Per serving: Calories 206, Protein 7g, Total Fat 11g, Cholesterol 5mg, Sodium 332mg, Total Carbohydrate 20g, Dietary Fiber 6g, Sugars 3g, Vitamin C 108%, Calcium 11%.

27. Shallot and garlic roasted cauliflower

This roasted cauliflower dish is flavored with shallot and garlic and takes only 20 minutes to prepare and cook. It makes a great side dish or healthy snack that is low in carbs and gluten-free.
Serving: 4-6
Preparation Time: 10 minutes
Ready Time: 20 minutes

Ingredients:
- 1 head of cauliflower (approx. 1.5 pounds, cut into florets)
- 2 tablespoons of olive oil
- 2 cloves of garlic (minced)
- 2 shallots (diced)
- Salt and pepper (to taste)

Instructions:
1. Preheat the oven to 450°F.
2. In a large bowl, mix together the cauliflower, olive oil, garlic, shallots, and salt and pepper until evenly combined.
3. Spread the cauliflower mixture onto a foil-lined baking sheet, spreading it out in a single layer.
4. Roast in the preheated oven for 18-20 minutes, stirring once halfway through, until the cauliflower is cooked through and lightly roasted.
5. Serve warm and enjoy!

Nutrition Information:
Serving size: 1/6 of the recipe
Calories: 62 kcal
Carbs: 7.4g
Fat: 3.4g
Protein: 2.4g
Fiber: 2.5g

28. Shallot and mushroom soup

Shallot and mushroom soup is a comforting and creamy soup that is so easy to make. It is packed full of flavor and comes together in no time.
Serving: 4
Preparation Time: 10 minutes

Ready Time: 25 minutes

Ingredients:
- 2 tablespoons olive oil
- 1/2 cup diced shallots
- 3 cloves garlic, minced
- 1 lb mushrooms, sliced
- 4 cups vegetable broth
- 1/4 cup heavy cream
- Salt and pepper, to taste

Instructions:
1. Heat the olive oil in a large pot over medium heat.
Add shallots and garlic and cook for 2 minutes.
2. Add mushrooms and cook until they soften and lose their liquid, about 8 minutes.
3. Pour in the vegetable broth and bring to a simmer.
Let cook for about 15 minutes.
4. Turn off the heat and carefully purée the soup with an immersion blender.
Alternatively, you can pour the soup into a blender and purée until smooth.
5. Stir in cream and season with salt and pepper to taste.

Nutrition Information (per serving): 247 cal, 17g fat, 13g carbs, 5g protein

29. Shallot and garlic roasted lamb chops

Our delicious Shallot and Garlic Roasted Lamb Chops are sure to be a hit amongst your family and friends. The marinade of garlic, shallots, and herbs will make this dish simply irresistible!
Serving: 4
Preparation Time: 10 minutes
Ready Time: 45 minutes

Ingredients:
• 4 lamb chops

- 6 cloves garlic, minced
- 2 shallots, thinly sliced
- 1/4 cup olive oil
- 2 tablespoons balsamic vinegar
- 2 tablespoons fresh parsley, chopped
- 1 teaspoon dried thyme
- Salt and pepper

Instructions:
1. Preheat oven to 425°F (220°C).
2. In a small bowl, whisk together olive oil, balsamic vinegar, garlic, shallots, parsley, thyme, salt, and pepper.
3. Place the lamb chops on a baking tray and cover with the marinade.
4. Roast in preheated oven for 15 minutes, then reduce heat to 350°F (180°C) and roast for an additional 25-30 minutes.
5. Serve immediately.

Nutrition Information: Calories: 302, Fat: 20g, Saturated Fat: 5g, Cholesterol: 66mg, Sodium: 164mg, Carbohydrates: 6g, Fiber: 1g, Sugar: 2g, Protein: 24g

30. Shallot and herb roasted turkey breast

Shallot and Herb Roasted Turkey Breast is a delicious and flavorful way to invigorate an ordinary turkey breast. This recipe will yield perfect, juicy slices of turkey that are filled with the complex flavors of shallots, thyme, and oregano.
Serving: 4
Preparation Time: 30 minutes
Ready Time: 1 hour

Ingredients:
2 lbs turkey breast
2 cloves garlic, minced
2 shallots, minced
1 tablespoon dried oregano
1 tablespoon dried thyme
2 tablespoons butter, melted

1 teaspoon freshly ground pepper

Instructions:
1. Preheat the oven to 350 degrees F.
2. Place the turkey breast in a baking dish.
3. In a small bowl, mix the garlic, shallots, oregano, thyme, melted butter, and fresh black pepper together.
4. Rub the mixture on the top and sides of the turkey breast until it is completely covered.
5. Place the turkey in the preheated oven and bake for approximately 50-60 minutes or until a meat thermometer reads 165 degrees F.
6. Once finished cooking, remove the turkey from the oven and let it rest about 10 minutes before slicing and serving.

Nutrition Information:
Calories: 270
Total Fat: 13g
Saturated Fat: 6g
Cholesterol: 97mg
Sodium: 108mg
Carbohydrates: 1g
Protein: 37g

31. Shallot and goat cheese stuffed mushrooms

Shallot and goat cheese stuffed mushrooms are an excellent appetizer or light main course. Loaded with savory shallots and earthy goat cheese, these mushrooms are sure to be a hit.
Serving: 6
Preparation Time: 15 minutes
Ready Time: 25 minutes

Ingredients:
- 12 large mushrooms, stalks removed
- 2 shallots, diced
- 4 ounces goat cheese
- 2 tablespoons olive oil
- 2 tablespoons parsley, chopped

- 1/2 teaspoon garlic powder
- Salt and pepper

Instructions:
1. Preheat oven to 375°F (190°C).
2. Place the mushroom caps in a greased baking dish.
3. In a small bowl, mix together the shallots, goat cheese, olive oil, parsley, garlic powder, salt, and pepper.
4. Stuff the mushroom caps with the shallot and goat cheese mixture.
5. Bake in preheated oven for 20 minutes, or until mushrooms are cooked through.

Nutrition Information:
Serving size: 2 mushrooms
Calories: 170
Fat: 13.5g
Carbohydrates: 5.3g
Protein: 6.3g

32. Shallot and herb roasted pork chops

This Shallot and Herb Roasted Pork Chops recipe is an easy yet delicious meal that your family will love. The tasty combination of shallots and herbs elevates the flavor of the pork chops for an unforgettable meal.
Serving: 4
Preparation Time: 10 minutes
Ready Time: 25 minutes

Ingredients:
- 4 bone-in pork chops
- 2 tablespoons olive oil
- 1 large shallot, thinly sliced
- 2 cloves garlic, minced
- 1 teaspoon dried oregano
- 1 teaspoon dried rosemary
- Salt and pepper to taste

Instructions:

1. Preheat oven to 350°F.
2. Grease a large baking dish with non-stick spray or olive oil.
3. Place pork chops in the dish.
4. In a small bowl, mix together olive oil, shallot, garlic, oregano, rosemary, salt and pepper.
5. Pour shallot mixture over pork chops and rub into the meat.
6. Bake in preheated oven for 25 minutes, or until pork reaches an internal temperature of 145°F.

Nutrition Information (per serving): 290 calories, 16g of fat, 3g of carbohydrates, 32g of protein.

33. Shallot and Parmesan roasted zucchini

This dish is a combination of two of the most delicious Ingredients – shallots and parmesan cheese—roasted zucchini. The combination of tartshallots and cheesy Parmesan gives the dish great flavor and mouthfeel.
Serving: 4
Preparation Time: 10 minutes
Ready Time: 25 minutes

Ingredients:
- 4 zucchinis, thickly sliced
- 2 Tbsp olive oil
- 2 shallots, diced
- 2 cloves of garlic, minced
- 2 Tbsp Parmesan cheese, grated
- Salt and pepper, to taste

Instructions:
1. Preheat oven to 400°F (200°C).
2. Line a baking sheet with parchment paper.
3. Place the sliced zucchinis on the baking sheet.
4. In a small bowl, mix together the olive oil, shallots, garlic, Parmesan cheese, and salt and pepper.
5. Pour the mixture over the zucchinis, making sure to evenly coat them.

6. Roast in the oven for 20-25 minutes, or until zucchinis are golden brown and tender.
7. Serve hot.

Nutrition Information: Per serving: 130 calories, 8 g fat, 2 g carbohydrates, 8 g protein, 2 g fiber, 102 mg sodium.

34. Shallot and bacon wrapped scallops

Treat yourself to a delicious and indulgent dinner of Shallot and Bacon Wrapped Scallops. The salty bacon pairs perfectly with the sweet shallots and the tender, juicy scallops, all cooked to perfection.
Serving: 4
Preparation Time: 10 minutes
Ready Time: 30 minutes

Ingredients:
-8 large scallops
-4 slices bacon, cut in half
-4 shallots, cut into chunks
-2 tablespoons of melted butter
-Salt and pepper to taste

Instructions:
1. Preheat oven to 375 degrees F.
2. Cut each bacon slice in half lengthwise. Wrap each scallop with a piece of bacon and secure with a toothpick if needed.
3. Arrange the wrapped scallops in a baking dish.
4. Top each scallop with a chunk of shallot and drizzle with melted butter.
5. Bake in the preheated oven for 30 minutes or until the bacon is cooked through and the shallots are tender.
6. Serve hot and enjoy!

Nutrition Information:
Calories: 176, Fat: 10g, Carbohydrate: 8g, Protein: 17g

35. Shallot and herb roasted rack of lamb

This Shallot and Herb Roasted Rack of Lamb recipe is a delicious and flavorful dinner that is sure to please a crowd. The combination of fresh herbs and shallot make a savory and juicy lamb rack that is perfectly cooked and melts in your mouth with every bite.

Serving: 6
Preparation Time: 10 minutes
Ready Time: 50 minutes

Ingredients:
- 2 racks of lamb
- 2 tablespoons of olive oil
- 2 shallots, finely chopped
- 2 cloves of garlic, minced
- 2 tablespoons of fresh rosemary, chopped
- 2 tablespoons of fresh thyme leaves
- 2 tablespoons of fresh oregano leaves
- 2 tablespoons of kosher salt
- 2 teaspoons of freshly ground black pepper

Instructions:
1. Preheat your oven to 350 degrees F.
2. In a small bowl, combine the minced garlic, shallots, rosemary, thyme, oregano, salt and black pepper.
3. Rub the herb mixture all over the lamb racks.
4. Heat a large skillet over medium heat. Once hot, add the olive oil.
5. Once the oil is hot, add the herb-coated racks of lamb. Sear each side for about 5 minutes, until golden brown.
6. Place the skillet in the preheated oven and roast for 35-40 minutes, until the internal temperature of the lamb reaches 145 degrees F.
7. Remove from the oven and let the racks rest for 10 minutes before slicing, to ensure the juiciest and most tender meat.

Nutrition Information:
Calories: 350, Fat: 25g, Carbs: 1g, Protein: 30g, cholesterol: 155mg, sodium: 1090mg

Shallot and garlic roasted prime rib is an easy but delicious dish that will satisfy even the most die-hard carnivore. It is a perfect festive entree for the family that is sure to delight!
Serving: 6
Preparation Time: 10 minutes
Ready Time: 2 hours 15 minutes

Ingredients:
-4-5 pound bone-in rib roast
-1 teaspoon whole black peppercorns
-3-4 sprigs fresh thyme
-2 tablespoons olive oil
-2 cloves garlic, minced
-2 shallots, thinly sliced
-Kosher salt

Instructions:
1. Get the oven ready to 375° F.
2. Rub the roast with olive oil and sprinkle liberally with kosher salt, black peppercorns and fresh thyme.
3. Place the roast on a roasting pan, surrounded by the minced garlic and shallots.
4. Roast in the preheated oven for 1 hour 45 minutes or until the roast reaches an internal temperature of 145-160° F
5. Allow the roast to rest for 10 minutes before slicing.

Nutrition Information:
Nutritional analysis per Serving: Calories: 518kcal, Carbs: 0g, Protein: 61g, Fat: 33g, Saturated fat: 12g, Cholesterol: 184mg, Sodium: 299mg, Potassium: 675mg, Fiber: 0g, Sugar: 0g, Vitamin A: 242IU, Vitamin C: 2mg, Calcium: 20mg, Iron: 3mg

37. Shallot and mushroom frittata

Shallot and Mushroom Frittata is an easy, hearty breakfast, lunch, or dinner dish that is packed with flavor.

Serving: 4
Preparation Time: 20 minutes
Ready Time: 45 minutes

Ingredients:
- 6 shallot cloves, minced
- 3 portobello mushrooms, thinly sliced
- 4 eggs
- 2 tablespoons olive oil
- ½ teaspoon freshly ground black pepper
- ½ teaspoon salt

Instructions:
1. Preheat oven to 350°F.
2. Heat oil in a 10 inch oven-safe skillet over medium-high heat.
3. Add shallots and mushrooms and cook, stirring frequently, until golden brown (approx 10 minutes).
4. Meanwhile, in a medium bowl, beat together eggs, salt, and pepper.
5. Add the egg mixture to skillet and stir to combine with shallots and mushrooms.
6. Reduce heat to medium and let cook until edges of the frittata begin to set (approx 5-7 minutes).
7. Place skillet in oven and bake for 20 minutes.
8. Remove from oven and let cool for 10-15 minutes before slicing and serving.

Nutrition Information: Calories 200, Total Fat 13.4g, Cholesterol 186mg, Sodium 570mg, Total Carbohydrates 7.2g, Dietary Fiber 2.2g, Protein 12.4g.

38. Shallot and garlic roasted salmon

This simple yet delicious roasted shallot and garlic salmon is the perfect way to enjoy a healthy dinner. Its quick and easy preparation allows you to have a tasty meal in a matter of minutes.
Serving: 4
Preparation time: 10 minutes
Ready time: 20 minutes

Ingredients:
- 4 (6oz) salmon filets
- 2 tablespoons olive oil
- ¾ teaspoon garlic powder
- ½ teaspoon onion powder
- ¼ teaspoon paprika
- Salt and pepper, to taste
- 1 large shallot, sliced

Instructions:
1. Preheat oven to 375°F (190°C).
2. Place the salmon filets in a greased baking dish and season with garlic powder, onion powder, paprika, salt and pepper.
3. Drizzle with olive oil and top with the sliced shallot.
4. Bake in preheated oven for 18-20 minutes, or until cooked through.

Nutrition Information (per serving):
Calories: 295, Fat: 16.8g, Saturated fat: 2.8g, Protein: 28.2g, Carbohydrate: 3.9g, Fiber: 0.6g, Sugar: 1.4g, Sodium: 142mg

39. Shallot and Parmesan roasted eggplant

Shallot and Parmesan Roasted Eggplant is a delicious side dish that pairs perfectly with a variety of main courses. It requires minimal Ingredients, and is relatively quick to make.
Serving: 2-3
Preparation time: 10 minutes
Ready time: 25 minutes

Ingredients:
- 2 large eggplants
- 2 cloves garlic, minced
- 2 shallots, minced
- ¼ cup olive oil
- ¼ cup grated Parmesan cheese
- 2 tablespoons freshly minced oregano
- Salt and pepper, to taste

Instructions:
1. Preheat your oven to 435°F.
2. Slice the eggplants into ¼-inch thick slices and lay them out flat on a greased baking sheet.
3. In a small bowl, combine the garlic, shallots, olive oil, Parmesan cheese and oregano. Mix until everything is well combined.
4. Use a pastry brush to brush the mixture onto the eggplants, coating both sides.
5. Sprinkle with salt and pepper, to taste.
6. Bake for 20-25 minutes, or until the eggplants are golden and tender.
7. Serve.

Nutrition Information (per serving):
Calories: 150, Fat: 11.4g, Carbohydrates: 8.2g, Protein: 4.3g, Sodium: 139mg

40. Shallot and herb roasted Cornish game hens

Shallot and Herb Roasted Cornish Game Hens
Serving: 4
Preparation time: 10 minutes
Ready time: 45 minutes

Ingredients:
• 2 1.5-pound Cornish Game Hens
• 2 tablespoons extra virgin olive oil
• 4 shallots, minced
• 2 minced garlic cloves
• Sea salt and ground black pepper, to taste
• 2 tablespoons freshly chopped rosemary, plus more for garnish
• 2 tablespoons freshly chopped oregano leaves, plus more for garnish

Instructions:
1. Preheat oven to 350°F.
2. Rub the hens with the olive oil and set aside.

3. Combine the shallots, garlic, salt, pepper, rosemary, and oregano in a bowl. Place hens on a parchment-lined baking sheet.

4. Fill the hollow of each hen with the shallot and herb mixture.

5. Spread the remaining mixture on the surface of the hens.

6. Roast the hens in preheated oven for 40-45 minutes, or until the internal temperature in the breast reaches 165°F and the juices run clear when pierced with a knife.

7. Remove hens from heat, loosely tent with foil, and let rest 10 minutes before serving.

8. Garnish with fresh rosemary and oregano.

Nutrition Information (per serving):
- 290 calories
- 22g fat
- 28g protein
- 2g carbohydrates
- 1g fiber

41. Shallot and goat cheese crostini

Shallot and goat cheese crostini
Serving: 4
Preparation time: 20 minutes
Ready Time: 45 minutes

Ingredients:
- 2 medium shallots, chopped
- 4 tablespoons olive oil
- 4 teaspoons balsamic vinegar
- ½ teaspoon sugar
- Salt and freshly ground black pepper, to taste
- 4 ounces fresh goat cheese
- 4 slices French or Italian-style baguette

Instructions:
1. Preheat the oven to 375°F (190°C).

2. In a small bowl, combine the chopped shallots, olive oil, balsamic vinegar, sugar, a pinch of salt and pepper, and stir until combined.

3. Spread the mixture evenly onto the slices of baguette. Top each slice with a few pieces of the goat cheese.
4. Place the crostini onto a baking sheet lined with parchment paper and bake in the preheated oven for 15-20 minutes or until golden brown and toasted.
5. Serve warm.

Nutrition Information: Per serving: 280 calories; 18 g fat; 8 g saturated fat; 10 g carbohydrates; 5 g protein; 500 mg sodium; 0.3 g fiber.

42. Shallot and herb roasted beef roast

This Shallot and Herb Roasted Beef Roast is an easy and tasty meal, perfect for a dinner or Sunday lunch. With the flavorful combination of Ingredients, it makes for a deliciously comforting and filling meal.
Serving: 4
Preparation Time: 15 minutes
Ready Time: 1 hour and 30 minutes

Ingredients:
- 2-3lb beef roast
- 2 large shallots, peeled and sliced
- 5 cloves garlic, minced
- 2 tablespoons of fresh rosemary, finely chopped
- 2 tablespoons of fresh thyme, finely chopped
- 2 tablespoons of olive oil
- Salt and pepper, to taste

Instructions:
1. Preheat oven to 350°F.
2. On a cutting board, sprinkle beef roast with salt, pepper, rosemary and thyme. Then, rub herbs into roast.
3. Heat oil in a large oven-safe skillet over medium-high heat.
4. Place roast in skillet and sear on all sides until nicely browned, about 5 minutes per side.
5. Move roast to a plate and set aside.

6. Add shallots and garlic to skillet and cook until fragrant, about 1-2 minutes.
7. Place beef roast back into skillet.
8. Place skillet in oven and roast until internal temperature reaches 145°F.
9. Let meat rest for 10 minutes before slicing.

Nutrition Information: Per serving, this Shallot and Herb Roasted Beef Roast is approximately 464 calories, 32 grams of fat, 1 gram of carbohydrates, and 39 grams of protein.

43. Shallot and Parmesan roasted carrots

Shallot and Parmesan roasted carrots is an easy and flavourful side dish that pairs perfectly with your favourite main course.
Serving: 4-6
Preparation Time: 10 minutes
Ready Time: 25 minutes

Ingredients:
• 1 lb carrots, peeled and thinly sliced
• 2 large shallots, thinly sliced
• 2 tablespoons olive oil
• 2 tablespoons freshly grated Parmesan cheese
• Salt and pepper, to taste
• 2 tablespoons freshly chopped parsley

Instructions:
1. Preheat oven to 400°F (200°C).
2. Toss carrots and shallots with olive oil and spread evenly on a baking sheet.
3. Roast for 20 minutes, stirring once halfway through.
4. Remove pan from oven, sprinkle Parmesan cheese, salt, and pepper on top.
5. Place back in oven for an additional 5 minutes or until carrots are golden and tender.
6. Serve warm, garnished with freshly chopped parsley.

Nutrition Information:

Calories: 66 kcal; Carbohydrates: 6 g; Protein: 2 g; Fat: 4 g; Cholesterol: 3 mg; Sodium: 128 mg; Potassium: 302 mg; Fiber: 2 g; Sugar: 3 g; Vitamin A: 17596 IU; Vitamin C: 6.7 mg; Calcium: 56 mg; Iron: 0.5 mg.

44. Shallot and bacon roasted green beans

Shallot and bacon roasted green beans - Serves 4, Preparation time 10 minutes, Ready in 40 minutes

Ingredients:
• 500g green beans, trimmed
• 3 shallots, peeled and finely sliced
• 4 rashers bacon, chopped into small pieces
• 2 tablespoons olive oil
• Salt and pepper

Instructions:
1. Preheat oven to 200°C (400°F).
2. Place green beans in a large bowl. Add shallots, bacon, and olive oil. Season with salt and pepper and mix until blended.
3. Spread on a baking sheet.
4. Bake for 30 minutes, or until beans are tender and bacon is crispy.

Nutrition Information (per serving):
• Calories: 135 kcal
• Carbohydrates: 7g
• Protein: 3g
• Fat: 10g
• Sodium: 180mg

45. Shallot and mushroom omelet

Shallot and mushroom omelet
Serving: 2
Preparation time: 10 minutes
Ready time: 15 minutes

Ingredients:
-2 shallots, diced
-2 mushrooms of your choice, diced
-3 eggs
-1 tablespoon of butter
-1 tablespoon of olive oil
-Pinch of fresh parsley, chopped
-Salt and pepper, to taste

Instructions:
1. Heat butter and olive oil in a large non stick skillet over medium heat.
2. Add shallots and mushrooms and cook until lightly browned, about 4 minutes.
3. Whisk eggs in a bowl and season with salt and pepper to taste.
4. Pour eggs into the skillet and stir briefly with a wooden spoon to combine the Ingredients together.
5. Allow eggs to cook until nearly all the liquid is gone, and stir in fresh parsley.
6. Flip the omelet and cook until the top is lightly browned.
7. Serve, enjoy!

Nutrition Information: Per Serving: 150 calories, 12 g of fat (mostly from the eggs), 4 g of carbohydrates, and 7 g of protein.

46. Shallot and garlic roasted swordfish

Shallot and garlic Roasted Swordfish
Serving: 4
Preparation time: 10 minutes
Ready time: 20 minutes

Ingredients:
- 4 (120 g) swordfish steaks
- 2 large shallots, diced
- 2 cloves garlic, minced
- 2 tablespoons olive oil
- 2 tablespoons lime juice

- 1 tablespoon chopped fresh parsley
- ½ teaspoon salt
- ¼ teaspoon pepper

Instructions:
1. Preheat oven to 400 degrees F (200 degrees C).
2. Place swordfish steaks in a baking dish.
3. In a small bowl, combine diced shallots, garlic, olive oil, lime juice, parsley, salt, and pepper. Mix well.
4. Pour mixture over the swordfish steaks, and turn to coat evenly.
5. Bake in preheated oven for 15 to 20 minutes, or until the swordfish flakes easily with a fork.

Nutrition Information:
Calories: 233 kcal, Carbohydrates: 5g, Protein: 21g, Fat: 14g, Saturated Fat: 2g, Cholesterol: 50mg, Sodium: 385mg, Potassium: 602mg, Fiber: 1g, Sugar: 1g, Vitamin A: 81IU, Vitamin C: 13mg, Calcium: 30mg, Iron: 1mg

47. Shallot and herb roasted quail

A mouthwatering dish, shallot and herb roasted quail is a true delight. The flavors of shallot, herbs, and quail come together to create a delectable dish that's sure to please.
Serving: 4
Preparation time: 10 minutes
Ready time: 40 minutes

Ingredients:
4 quail
2 shallots, peeled and finely diced
2 cloves of garlic, finely chopped
6 tablespoons of butter
2 tablespoons of fresh parsley
2 tablespoons of fresh thyme
Salt and pepper, to taste

Instructions:
1.Preheat the oven to 400F and grease a baking tray.

2.In a bowl, mix together the shallots, garlic, butter, parsley, thyme, salt, and pepper.

3.Rub the mixture all over each quail.

4.Place the quail onto the prepared baking tray and place in the oven.

5.Bake at 400F for 30 minutes, or until the quail is cooked through and golden brown.

6.Remove the quail from the oven and serve immediately.

Nutrition Information: Per serving (1 Quail): Calories: 208 Protein: 12g Fat: 17g Carbs: 0g Fiber: 0g Sodium: 390mg

48. Shallot and Parmesan roasted sweet potatoes

Shallot and Parmesan Roasted Sweet Potatoes
Serving: 4
Preparation time: 10 minutes
Ready time: 30 minutes

Ingredients:
- 2 large sweet potatoes
- 2 tablespoons olive oil
- 2 garlic cloves, minced
- 2 tablespoons shallots, chopped
- 2 tablespoons fresh thyme leaves
- 2 tablespoons grated Parmesan cheese
- Salt and pepper, to taste

Instructions:
1. Preheat oven to 400°F.
2. Peel and cut the sweet potatoes into small cubes.
3. In a large bowl, combine the sweet potatoes, olive oil, garlic, shallots, thyme and Parmesan cheese. Mix until all the cubes are evenly coated.
4. Spread out the mixture onto a large baking sheet.
5. Roast for 25–30 minutes, until the sweet potatoes are golden and tender.
6. Serve warm.

Nutrition Information per Serving (4 servings):

Calories: 155, Total Fat: 7.5g, Sodium: 128mg, Carbohydrates: 19.8g, Fiber: 3.1g, Sugar: 4g, Protein: 3.5g

49. Shallot and goat cheese pizza

Shallot and Goat Cheese Pizza
Serving: 4
Preparation Time: 15 minutes
Ready Time: 45 minutes

Ingredients:
-1 (12 to 16-ounce) prebaked thin pizza crust
-1/3 cup olive oil
-3 medium shallots, very thinly sliced
-1/2 teaspoon salt
-1/4 teaspoon freshly ground black pepper
-2 to 3 ounces soft chèvre (goat cheese), crumbled
-1 cup finely grated smoked Gouda or Gruyère cheese
-1/4 cup freshly grated Parmesan cheese (optional)

Instructions:
1. Preheat oven to 375°F.
2. Place the pizza crust on a baking sheet.
3. In a medium bowl, combine the olive oil, shallots, salt, and pepper.
4. Spread the shallot mixture evenly over the pizza crust.
5. Sprinkle the crumbled goat cheese, smoked Gouda, and Parmesan (if using) over the pizza.
6. Bake for 20 to 25 minutes, or until the cheese is melted and bubbly.
7. Cut into slices and serve.

Nutrition Information:
Calories: 365, Fat: 21 g, Carbohydrates: 28 g, Protein: 13 g, Sodium: 682 mg

50. Shallot and herb roasted leg of lamb

This Shallot and Herb Roasted Leg of Lamb is a succulent and decadent dish that is perfect for a special occasion. The fragrant smell of roasted herbs and shallots will fill your home with unbelievable aromas and the flavors will be unforgettable.

Serving: Serves 8
Preparation Time: 15 minutes
Ready Time: 90 minutes

Ingredients:
- 5-pound leg of lamb
- 2 tablespoons olive oil
- 5 cloves garlic, minced
- 1/2 teaspoon salt
- 1/4 teaspoon black pepper
- 1 large shallot, sliced
- 1/4 cup fresh rosemary
- 2 tablespoons fresh thyme
- 2 tablespoons fresh oregano

Instructions:
1. Preheat oven to 375 degrees F.
2. In a small bowl, mix together olive oil, garlic, salt, and pepper.
3. Place the leg of lamb on a roasting pan. Rub the mixture all over the surface of the lamb.
4. Arrange the shallots, rosemary, thyme, and oregano on top of the lamb.
5. Roast in preheated oven for about 1 1/2 hours, or until the internal temperature reaches 125 degrees F for medium rare.
6. Let rest for 10 minutes before carving.

Nutrition Information: Per serving: 335 calories, 22.8 g protein, 25.7 g fat, 3.7 g carbohydrates, 0 g fiber, 1.2 g sugar, 62 mg cholesterol, 251 mg sodium

51. Shallot and garlic roasted shrimp

Shallot and Garlic Roasted Shrimp is a flavorful dish that packs a punch of zesty aromas from the roasted shallots and garlic. It's a quick and easy dinner dish that is perfect for any weeknight meal.

Serving: 4
Preparation Time: 10 minutes
Ready Time: 25 minutes

Ingredients:
- 1 ½ pounds large shrimp, peeled and deveined
- 3 tablespoons extra-virgin olive oil
- 1 cup very thinly sliced shallots
- 6 garlic cloves, minced
- 1 tablespoon minced fresh parsley
- 1 teaspoon chopped fresh thyme
- ½ teaspoon salt
- Freshly ground pepper to taste

Instructions:
1. Preheat oven to 425°F.
2. Place the shrimp in a large bowl. Add the oil, shallots, garlic, parsley, thyme, salt and pepper, and gently toss together.
3. Transfer the shrimp to a 10-by-15-inch roasting pan. Roast, stirring once, until the shrimp are opaque throughout, 15 to 20 minutes.
4. Serve warm.

Nutrition Information: Per serving (4 servings): 228 calories; 8 g fat (1 g sat, 6 g mono); 143 mg cholesterol; 5 g carbohydrate; 24 g protein; 0 g fiber; 270 mg sodium; 108 mg potassium.

52. Shallot and bacon quinoa salad

Shallot and Bacon Quinoa Salad
Serving: 8
Preparation Time: 15 minutes
Ready Time: 25 minutes

Ingredients:
- 2 cups vegetable broth

- 1 cup uncooked quinoa
- 6 strips of bacon, cooked and chopped
- 4 large shallots, diced
- 2 tablespoons freshly chopped parsley
- 2 tablespoons freshly chopped chives
- 2 tablespoons freshly chopped dill
- 2 tablespoons freshly squeezed lemon juice
- ½ teaspoon sea salt
- ½ teaspoon black pepper

Instructions:
1. In a medium saucepan, bring vegetable broth to a boil.
2. Add quinoa and stir. Reduce heat to low, cover, and simmer for 10 minutes until the liquid is absorbed.
3. Remove from heat and let stand for 5 minutes. Fluff with a fork.
4. In a large bowl, add cooked quinoa, bacon, shallots, parsley, chives, dill, lemon juice, salt, and pepper. Mix until combined.
5. Serve warm or cold.

Nutrition Information:
Calories: 222
Carbohydrates: 16.7 grams
Protein: 8.2 grams
Fat: 11.9 grams
Saturated fat: 3.6 grams
Cholesterol: 18 mg
Sodium: 471 mg
Potassium: 202 mg
Fiber: 2.2 grams
Sugar: 1.3 grams

53. Shallot and mushroom ragout

Shallot and Mushroom Ragout
Serving: 4
Preparation Time: 10 minutes
Ready Time: 25 minutes

Ingredients:
- 2 tablespoons olive oil
- 2 large shallots, chopped
- 2 cloves garlic, minced
- 8 ounces fresh mushrooms, sliced
- 2 tablespoons all-purpose flour
- 1/2 teaspoon dried thyme
- 1/4 teaspoon salt
- 1/8 teaspoon freshly ground black pepper
- 1 cup chicken broth
- 2 tablespoons dry white wine
- 2 tablespoons finely chopped fresh parsley

Instructions:
1.Heat the oil in a large skillet over medium heat. Add the shallots and garlic and sauté for 2-3 minutes until shallots are translucent.
2.Add the mushrooms and sauté for 4-5 minutes until mushrooms are golden brown. Stir in the flour, thyme, salt, and pepper and mix until combined.
3.Stir in the chicken broth and wine and bring to a simmer. Simmer for 10-12 minutes until sauce is thick and bubbly.
4.Stir in the fresh parsley and season with additional salt and pepper to taste.

Nutrition Information:
Calories: 113, Fat: 7 g, Saturated Fat: 1 g, Cholesterol: 0 mg, Sodium: 289 mg, Carbohydrates: 9 g, Fiber: 1 g, Sugar: 2 g, Protein: 4 g
This Shallot and Mushroom Ragout is a flavorful and easy side dish that comes together in just 25 minutes. It's made with shallots, mushrooms, garlic, flour, and herbs and spices for a savory and delicious meal. Enjoy with a side of mashed potatoes or over hot cooked pasta for a quick and delicious dinner!

54. Shallot and garlic roasted duck breast

Shallot and garlic roasted duck breast
Serving: 4
Preparation Time: 10 minutes

Ready Time: 45 minutes

Ingredients:
- 4 duck breasts
- 4 cloves of garlic
- 2 tablespoons of olive oil
- Salt and pepper to season
- 5 shallots, peeled and diced
- 2 tablespoons of honey

Instructions:
1. Preheat the oven to 375°F.
2. Acrub the duck breasts with the garlic, then drizzle the olive oil over the top.
3. Sprinkle with salt and pepper to season.
4. Place the duck breasts in a roasting tray and cover with the diced shallots.
5. Roast in the oven for 20 minutes, then remove and drizzle the honey over the top.
6. Return the duck to the oven and continue cooking for a further 25 minutes.
7. When cooked, remove the duck breasts from the roasting tray and let them rest for 10 minutes before serving.

Nutrition Information (per serving):
- Calories: 295
- Fat: 21.7 g
- Carbohydrates: 5.6 g
- Protein: 21.1 g
- Sodium: 104 mg

55. Shallot and herb roasted beef ribs

Shallot and Herb Roasted Beef Ribs
Serving: 6
Preparation Time: 15 minutes
Ready Time: 1 hour 15 minutes

Ingredients:
- 2 pounds beef ribs
- 2 shallots, quartered
- 2 tablespoons fresh chopped herbs, such as rosemary, thyme, oregano and parsley
- 2 tablespoons olive oil
- 2 cloves garlic, minced
- Salt and pepper to taste

Instructions:
1. Preheat oven to 400°F. Place beef ribs in a roasting dish.
2. In a small bowl, combine olive oil, garlic, herbs, shallots, and salt and pepper to taste.
3. Rub the mixture on both sides of the ribs.
4. Place the ribs on a roasting pan and cover with foil.
5. Roast for 45 minutes and then remove the foil.
6. Continue to roast for 20-25 minutes more or until the ribs are cooked through.
7. Let the ribs rest for 10 minutes before serving.

Nutrition Information (per serving):
Calories: 298, Total Fat: 15 g, Saturated Fat: 4 g, Cholesterol: 131 mg, Sodium: 77 mg, Potassium: 519 mg, Total Carbohydrate: 1 g, Dietary Fiber: 0 g, Protein: 33 g

56. Shallot and Parmesan roasted squash

This roasted squash dish is an easy yet flavorful side perfect for any meal – bursting with Parmesan and shallot flavors.
Serving: Serves 4
Preparation Time: 10 minutes
Ready Time: 40 minutes

Ingredients:
- 2 lb small squash, such as acorn, cut into 1/2-inch-thick slices
- 2 tablespoons extra-virgin olive oil
- 2 tablespoons chopped shallot
- 1/4 teaspoon chili flakes

- 2 tablespoons finely grated Parmigiano-Reggiano cheese
- Kosher salt

Instructions:
1. Preheat oven to 375°F.
2. Toss squash with olive oil, shallot and chili flakes in a large bowl.
3. Spread squash in a single layer on a rimmed baking sheet. Sprinkle with Parmesan and season with salt.
4. Roast squash, stirring once, until golden and tender, about 40 minutes.

Nutrition Information: Per serving: 130 cal, 10g fat (2g sat fat), 6g carbs, 4g protein, 3g fiber, 225mg sodium.

57. Shallot and goat cheese stuffed chicken breasts

Shallot and Goat Cheese Stuffed Chicken Breasts

Serving: 4
Preparation Time: 10 minutes
Ready Time: 40 minutes

Ingredients:
- 4 boneless, skinless chicken breasts
- 2 shallots, finely diced
- 2 tablespoons olive oil
- 4 ounces goat cheese
- Salt and pepper to taste

Instructions:
1. Preheat oven to 350 degrees F.
2. Place chicken breasts on a baking sheet and season with salt and pepper.
3. In a small frying pan, heat the olive oil and sauté the shallots until softened, about 2 minutes.
4. Remove from heat and let cool.
5. In a medium bowl, combine the goat cheese and shallots.
6. Place the chicken breasts on a cutting board and use a sharp knife to cut a deep pocket into each one.

7. Spoon the goat cheese and shallot mixture into the pockets.
8. Place the chicken breasts back on the baking sheet.
9. Bake for 40 minutes or until the chicken is cooked through.

Nutrition Information:
Calories: 449, Total fat: 24g, Saturated fat: 11g, Cholesterol: 160mg,
Sodium: 341mg, Carbohydrates: 3g, Protein: 55g, Fiber: 0g.

58. Shallot and herb roasted whole chicken

This shallot and herb roasted whole chicken is a classic home-cooked
meal that is perfect for the holidays. The combination of shallots, garlic,
rosemary and thyme create an aromatic and flavorful dish that will be
sure to please.
Serving: 4-6
Preparation Time: 10 minutes
Ready Time: 1 hour

Ingredients:
- 1 whole chicken, about 3 to 4 pounds
- 2 tablespoons olive oil
- 2 shallots, minced
- 4 cloves garlic, minced
- 1 teaspoon dried rosemary
- 1 teaspoon dried thyme
- Salt and pepper to taste

Instructions:
1. Preheat the oven to 375F (190C).
2. In a small bowl, mix together the olive oil, shallots, garlic, rosemary,
and thyme. Season with salt and pepper.
3. Place the chicken in a roasting pan. Rub the herb and shallot mixture
on and inside the chicken.
4. Roast the chicken for 45 minutes to 1 hour, until golden and cooked
through.
5. Remove the chicken from the oven, cover with foil and let rest for 10
minutes before carving.

Nutrition Information:
Calories: 350
Total Fat: 25 g
Saturated Fat: 7 g
Cholesterol: 90 mg
Sodium: 100 mg
Carbohydrates: 2 g
Protein: 28 g

59. Shallot and garlic roasted sea bass

Shallot and garlic roasted sea bass is a delicious and healthy dish. Its bold flavors come from the combination of shallot and garlic. It's an easy meal to prepare that can be ready in minutes.
Serving: 4-6
Preparation Time: 10 minutes
Ready Time: 40 minutes

Ingredients:
- 4-6 sea bass fillets
- 2 cloves garlic, minced
- 2 shallots, minced
- 3 tablespoons olive oil
- 2 teaspoons fresh thyme leaves
- 1 teaspoon sea salt
- ½ teaspoon freshly ground black pepper

Instructions:
1. Preheat oven to 400°F (200°C).
2. In a small bowl, mix together garlic, shallots, olive oil, thyme, sea salt and pepper.
3. Place sea bass fillets in a single layer on a baking sheet.
4. Spread the garlic and shallot mixture on top of the fillets.
5. Bake in preheated oven for 25-30 minutes until fish is cooked through.

Nutrition Information: Per serving: Calories: 206, Fat: 10.6g, Protein: 24.3g, Carbs: 1.1g, Sodium: 612mg

60. Shallot and mushroom ravioli

This classic Italian dish combines the delicious flavors of shallot and mushroom with pillowy ravioli, for a delightful dish that can be served as a main or side.
Serving: 8
Preparation Time: 20 minutes
Ready Time: 40 minutes

Ingredients:
- 12 ounces fresh or frozen ravioli
- 2 tablespoons butter
- 3 shallots, sliced
- 8 ounces mushrooms, sliced
- 2 cloves garlic, minced
- 2 tablespoons fresh thyme
- 2 tablespoons freshly grated parmesan cheese
- 2 tablespoons fresh parsley, chopped

Instructions:
1. Bring a large pot of salted water to a boil. Add ravioli and cook for 2-3 minutes or until al dente. Drain and set aside.
2. In a large skillet over medium-high heat, melt butter. Add shallots and mushrooms and cook for about 5 minutes, stirring occasionally.
3. Add garlic, thyme, and parmesan cheese and cook for 1 minute more, stirring to combine.
4. Add ravioli to the skillet and stir to combine. Add parsley, season to taste with salt and pepper, and cook for 1 minute more.

Nutrition Information:
Serving Size: 1/8 of recipe | Calories: 225 kcal | Carbohydrates: 19g | Protein: 5.7g | Fat: 13.6g | Saturated Fat: 7.4g | Cholesterol: 33.2mg | Sodium: 359mg | Potassium: 305.3mg | Fiber: 2.2g | Sugar: 1.3g | Vitamin A: 478.7IU | Vitamin C: 2.2mg | Calcium: 91.4mg | Iron: 1.1mg

Shallot and Bacon Stuffed Artichokes - Deliciously savory and hearty, this stuffed artichoke dish is sure to be an instant hit with your family and friends!
Serving: 4-6
Preparation Time: 15 minutes
Ready Time: 1 hour

Ingredients:
- 4 large artichokes
- 2 shallots, diced
- 4 slices bacon, cooked and crumbled
- 1/2 cup freshly grated Parmesan cheese
- 2 tablespoons olive oil
- 1 lemon, juiced
- 1/2 teaspoon garlic powder
- Salt and black pepper to taste

Instructions:
1. Preheat oven to 375°F.
2. Cut stems off of artichokes and remove any tough outer leaves.
3. In a medium bowl, combine shallots, bacon, Parmesan cheese, olive oil, lemon juice, garlic powder, salt and pepper.
4. Stuff artichokes with mixture and place in a greased 9x13-inch baking dish.
5. Drizzle artichokes with a bit of olive oil and lemon juice and season with salt and pepper.
6. Cover dish and bake for 30 minutes.
7. Uncover and bake for an additional 30 minutes, or until artichokes are tender.

Nutrition Information:
Calories: 123, Fat: 7 grams, Carbohydrates: 7 grams, Protein: 8 grams, Sodium: 221 mg

62. Shallot and herb roasted pork tenderloin

This classic pork tenderloin recipe is a simple and easy way to elevate a weeknight dinner, combining succulent and juicy pork tenderloin with a classic combination of shallot, herbs, and a delicious balsamic glaze.
Serving: Serves 8
Preparation Time: 15 minutes
Ready Time: 1 hour and 10 minutes

Ingredients:
- 2 lb pork tenderloin
- 2 shallots, thinly sliced
- 2 Tablespoons fresh rosemary, minced
- 2 Tablespoons fresh thyme, minced
- 2 garlic cloves, finely minced
- 2 Tablespoons olive oil
- 3 Tablespoons balsamic glaze or reduced balsamic vinegar
- Kosher salt and freshly ground black pepper, to taste

Instructions:
1. Preheat oven to 375°F.
2. Place pork tenderloin on a baking sheet.
3. In a small bowl, combine shallots, rosemary, thyme, garlic, and olive oil. Rub the mixture onto the pork tenderloin.
4. Drizzle the balsamic glaze over the pork tenderloin and season with salt and pepper.
5. Bake in the preheated oven for 50-60 minutes, or until pork is cooked through.
6. Let pork rest for 10 minutes before slicing.

Nutrition Information: Calories: 176 kcal; Protein: 24 g; Fat: 7 g; Saturated Fat: 2 g; Cholesterol: 72 mg; Sodium: 110 mg; Potassium: 473 mg; Vitamin A: 2.2%; Vitamin C: 4.6%; Calcium: 1.9%; Iron: 5.4%

63. Shallot and Parmesan roasted beets

Shallot and Parmesan Roasted Beets are an easy-to-make, delicious side dish. This healthy dish is full of flavor and packed with nutrients like

iron, potassium, and fiber. Serve it up as a side dish or make it the star of your next meal.
Serving: 4-6
Preparation Time: 15 minutes
Ready Time: 40 minutes

Ingredients:
-3 large beets (about 1 pound), peeled and cut into 1-inch cubes
-1 tablespoons olive oil
-2 shallots, chopped
-2 cloves garlic, minced
-2 tablespoons balsamic vinegar
-1 tablespoon agave nectar
-Salt and pepper to taste
-2 tablespoons freshly grated Parmesan cheese

Instructions:
1. Preheat oven to 375°F.
2. In a large bowl, combine beets with the olive oil, shallots, garlic, balsamic vinegar, agave nectar, and salt and pepper.
3. Toss to combine.
4. Transfer mixture to a baking dish and roast in preheated oven for 30-35 minutes.
5. Remove the dish from the oven and top with Parmesan cheese. Return to oven and bake for an additional 5 minutes, or until cheese is melted and bubbly.
6. Serve warm.

Nutrition Information:
Calories: 91
Fat: 4g
Carbohydrates: 11g
Protein: 2g
Fiber: 2g
Sugar: 6g

64. Shallot and goat cheese stuffed bell peppers

Shallot and Goat Cheese Stuffed Bell Peppers are a delicious vegetarian dish packed with flavor. This dish is a great way to get your daily veggies and calcium. Serve this dish with a simple side salad or roasted potatoes for a complete meal.

Serving: 4
Preparation Time: 30 minutes
Ready Time: 1 hour

Ingredients:
- 4 bell peppers
- 2 shallots, diced
- 4oz of soft goat cheese
- 1 tablespoon of olive oil
- A handful of cherry tomatoes, halved
- 1 teaspoon of fresh thyme leaves
- Salt and pepper

Instructions:
1. Preheat your oven to 350F.
2. Slice the bell peppers in half and remove the seeds.
3. In a frying pan, heat the olive oil and add the shallots. Sauté until golden.
4. Add the cherry tomatoes and sauté for 1-2 minutes.
5. In a bowl, mix together the goat cheese, thyme, salt, and pepper.
6. Stuff each bell pepper half with the goat cheese mixture.
7. Place the bell peppers on a baking sheet and bake in the preheated oven for 25-30 minutes.

Nutrition Information per Serving: Calories: 280
Fat: 18g
Carbohydrates: 17g
Protein: 12g
Sodium: 372mg

65. Shallot and garlic roasted trout

This shallot and garlic roasted trout is flavourful and succulent; it's a quick and easy way to bring a delicious midday or evening meal to the table.

Serving: Serves 4
Preparation Time: 15 minutes
Ready Time: 25 minutes

Ingredients:
- 4 trout fillets
- 4 shallots, thinly sliced
- 4 garlic cloves, finely chopped
- 3 tablespoons olive oil
- 1 lemon, cut into wedges
- Salt and pepper to season

Instructions:
1. Preheat the oven to 200 degrees C.
2. Arrange the trout fillets in an oven-safe dish.
3. Top with the sliced shallots and chopped garlic.
4. Drizzle with the olive oil and season with salt and pepper.
5. Bake in the preheated oven for 20 minutes or until the fish is cooked through.
6. Serve with lemon wedges.

Nutrition Information:
Calories: 166, Fat: 9.7g, Carbohydrates: 1.2g, Protein: 17.6g, Sodium: 123mg, Potassium: 319mg

66. Shallot and herb roasted venison

Shallot and Herb Roasted Venison - An elegant and flavorful dish that packs plenty of protein, this shallot and herb roasted venison is sure to please a crowd.

Serving: 4
Preparation Time: 20 minutes
Ready Time: 1 hour

Ingredients:

- 3 pounds red deer meat, cut into cubes
- 4 tablespoons dried rosemary
- 2 tablespoons dried thyme
- 2 tablespoons garlic powder
- 2 tablespoons olive oil
- 4 shallots, finely chopped
- Salt and pepper, to taste

Instructions:
1. Preheat oven to 350 degrees F (175 degrees C).
2. In a large bowl, mix together rosemary, thyme, garlic powder, olive oil, shallots, salt, and pepper.
3. Add deer meat cubes to the bowl and toss until coated in the mixture.
4. Spread the meat and shallot mixture onto a parchment-lined baking sheet.
5. Bake in preheated oven for 30 minutes, or until the meat is cooked through.

Nutrition Information: Serving Size 4, Calories: 570, Total Fat: 23g, Cholesterol: 199mg, Sodium: 120mg, Total Carbohydrates: 2g, Protein: 84g.

67. Shallot and bacon deviled eggs

Shallot and Bacon Deviled Eggs are a classic twist on the traditional deviled eggs. Rich and creamy with pieces of shallot and bacon, these will be a hit at any gathering.
Serving: 6-8
Preparation Time: 10 minutes
Ready Time: 40 minutes

Ingredients:
- 8 large eggs
- 2 tablespoons mayonnaise
- 1 teaspoon Dijon mustard
- 1/4 teaspoon salt
- 1/4 teaspoon freshly ground black pepper
- 2 tablespoons finely chopped cooked bacon

- 2 tablespoons finely chopped shallots

Instructions:
1. Place the eggs in a single layer in a large saucepan. Fill with cold water to about 1 inch above the eggs.
2. Bring to a boil over medium-high heat, then remove the pan from the heat and let the eggs sit in the hot water for 14 minutes.
3. Transfer eggs to an ice water bath until cool to the touch.
4. Peel eggs and slice in half lengthwise; gently remove the yolks and place in a medium bowl.
5. Add mayonnaise, mustard, salt, pepper, bacon and shallots to the bowl and mix together well.
6. Spoon or pipe yolk mixture back into the hollowed eggs.
7. Serve chilled.

Nutrition Information:
Serving size: 1 egg (21 g)
Calories: 67 calories
Total Fat: 5 g
Saturated Fat: 1 g
Trans Fat: 0 g
Cholesterol: 61 mg
Sodium: 92 mg
Total Carbohydrate: 1 g
Dietary Fiber: 0 g
Sugars: 0 g
Protein: 4 g

68. Shallot and mushroom gravy

Enjoy a savory and rich shallot and mushroom gravy as a side for mashed potatoes, vegetables, and other traditional staples! This simple recipe can be made in about 25 minutes and is sure to be a hit among your family and friends.
Serving: Serves 4
Preparation Time: 10 minutes
Ready Time: 25 minutes

Ingredients:
- 2 tablespoons olive oil
- 1 shallot, diced
- 1 garlic clove, finely chopped
- 8 ounces mushrooms, sliced
- 2 tablespoons all-purpose flour
- 2 cups vegetable broth
- 2 tablespoons soy sauce
- 2 tablespoons Worcestershire sauce
- Salt and pepper to taste

Instructions:
1. Heat the oil in a large skillet over medium heat.
2. Add the shallot and garlic and cook for 1 minute.
3. Add the mushrooms and cook for about 4 minutes, until they are softened.
4. Sprinkle flour over the vegetables and stir to combine.
5. Pour in the vegetable broth, soy sauce, and Worcestershire sauce and stir to combine.
6. Bring the mixture to a boil and reduce to a simmer.
7. Simmer for 8 minutes, or until the sauce has thickened.
8. Season with salt and pepper, to taste.
9. Serve over mashed potatoes, vegetables, or your favorite dish.

Nutrition Information:
Calories: 89 kcal, Carbohydrates: 7.6 g, Protein: 2.6 g, Fat: 6 g, Saturated Fat: 0.9 g, Sodium: 693 mg, Potassium: 252 mg, Fiber: 1.3 g, Sugar: 1.4 g, Vitamin A: 25 IU, Vitamin C: 4 mg, Calcium: 8 mg, Iron: 1.2 mg

69. Shallot and garlic roasted quail

Shallot and garlic roasted quail is a delicious and savory dish, with an intense flavor. With roasted garlic, shallots and quail, it's a hearty meal that's sure to satisfy both your taste buds and your appetite!
Serving: 2
Preparation Time: 15 minutes
Ready Time: 35 minutes

Ingredients:
- 2 quails
- 2 cloves of garlic, minced
- 2 shallots, diced
- 2 tablespoons olive oil
- Salt and pepper to taste

Instructions:
1. Preheat your oven to 375°F (190°C).
2. In a small bowl, mix together the garlic, shallot, olive oil, salt and pepper.
3. Rub the mixture onto the quails and place in a greased baking dish.
4. Place the dish in the preheated oven and bake for 25 minutes or until the quail is cooked through.
5. Serve hot with your favorite side dishes.

Nutrition Information:
Calories: 295 kcal, Carbohydrates: 4.9 g, Protein: 22 g, Fat: 19.5 g, Saturated Fat: 4 g, Cholesterol: 78 mg, Sodium: 307 mg, Potassium: 319 mg, Fiber: 0.7 g, Sugar: 0.5 g, Vitamin A: 139 IU, Vitamin C: 2.8 mg, Calcium: 27 mg, Iron: 1.6 mg

70. Shallot and Parmesan roasted fennel

Shallot and Parmesan Roasted Fennel
Serving: 4
Preparation Time: 10 minutes
Ready Time: 40 minutes

Ingredients:
- 2 medium fennel bulbs
- 2 tablespoons extra virgin olive oil
- 2 shallots, thinly sliced
- 2 garlic cloves, finely chopped
- 2 tablespoons freshly grated Parmesan cheese
- Salt and freshly ground black pepper

Instructions:

1. Preheat oven to 350°F (175°C).
2. Cut the fennel bulb into quarters and remove the core. Cut the quarters in to slices.
3. Place slices into a baking dish and drizzle with olive oil, shallots, garlic, Parmesan cheese, salt, and pepper.
4. Cover with foil and bake for 30 minutes.
5. Remove foil and bake for an additional 10 minutes to brown the top of the fennel.

Nutrition Information:
Calories: 186
Total Fat: 11.5g
Total Carbohydrates: 16.3g
Protein: 5.9g
Cholesterol: 7mg
Sodium: 252mg

71. Shallot and goat cheese stuffed zucchini

Try our Shallot and Goat Cheese Stuffed Zucchini recipe and enjoy a delicious vegetarian dish! This crowd-pleasing recipe is made with zucchini, shallot, garlic, and goat cheese, and is full of flavorful Ingredients.
Serving: 4 servings
Preparation time: 15 minutes
Ready time: 35 minutes

Ingredients:
– 2 zucchinis
– 1 shallot, diced
– 2 cloves garlic, minced
– 2 tablespoons olive oil
– 2 ounces crumbled goat cheese
– 2 tablespoons chopped fresh parsley
– Salt and pepper to taste

Instructions:
1. Preheat the oven to 350°F.

2. Cut the zucchinis in half lengthwise and scoop out the middle, creating 4 boat-shaped halves. Place them on a baking sheet.

3. In a medium skillet, heat the olive oil over medium heat. Add the shallot and garlic and sauté for 3 minutes.

4. In a medium bowl, combine the cooked shallot and garlic with the goat cheese, parsley, salt, and pepper.

5. Spoon the mixture evenly into each zucchini boat.

6. Bake in the oven for 20 minutes, or until the zucchini is cooked through.

7. Serve warm and enjoy.

Nutrition Information:
Each serving contains 96 calories, 7 g fat, 2 g saturated fat, 2 g carbohydrates, 4 g protein, and 0 g fiber.

72. Shallot and herb roasted game hen

Shallot and Herb Roasted Game Hens are roasted chicken dish bursting with aromatic flavors of shallots, herbs, and butter. This recipe is perfect for a weeknight dinner and can easily be adjusted to accommodate any number of people.
Serving: 2
Preparation Time: 10 minutes
Ready Time: 50 minutes

Ingredients:
-2 game hens
-4 tablespoons butter, melted
-2 tablespoons olive oil
-1 large shallot, finely chopped
-1 tablespoon dried thyme
-1 teaspoon dried rosemary
-1 teaspoon dried oregano
-1/2 teaspoon ground black pepper
-1/2 teaspoon sea salt

Instructions:
1. Preheat oven to 375 degrees F (190 degrees C).

2. Place game hens in a roasting pan.

3. In a small bowl, mix together butter, olive oil, shallot, thyme, rosemary, oregano, black pepper, and salt.

4. Brush game hens with the butter mixture.

5. Roast in the preheated oven for 40-50 minutes, turning occasionally, until the juices run clear and the hens are golden and crispy.

Nutrition Information:

Calories: 584kcal, Carbohydrates: 1g, Protein: 28g, Fat: 52g, Saturated Fat: 20g, Cholesterol: 233mg, Sodium: 250mg, Potassium: 397mg, Sugar: 1g, Vitamin A: 1013IU, Vitamin C: 4mg, Calcium: 41mg, Iron: 2mg.

73. Shallot and garlic roasted halibut

Enjoy a perfectly seasoned and oven-baked Halibut dinner with this Shallot and Garlic Roasted Halibut recipe.

Serving: 4 people

Preparation Time: 10 minutes

Ready Time: 25 minutes

Ingredients:
- 4 (4 ounces) halibut fillets
- 2 tablespoons olive oil
- 2 tablespoons butter
- 1/2 shallot, chopped
- 2 cloves garlic, minced
- 1/2 teaspoon Italian seasoning
- 1/2 teaspoon dried parsley
- 1/4 teaspoon paprika
- Salt and pepper to taste

Instructions:

1. Preheat the oven to 375 degrees F. Line a baking sheet with parchment paper and set aside.

2. In a medium bowl, whisk together the olive oil, butter, shallot, garlic, Italian seasoning, parsley, paprika, salt and pepper.

3. Place the halibut fillets on the parchment paper and brush them with the olive oil mixture.

4. Bake for 20-25 minutes, or until the fish is cooked through.
5. Serve with your favorite vegetables or side dish.

Nutrition Information: Per serving (4 ounces): Calories-211, Protein-27.2g, Fat-10.4g, Carbs-0.3g, Fiber-0.3g, Sugar-0g, Cholesterol-44mg, Sodium-171mg.

74. Shallot and bacon mac and cheese

Shallot and bacon mac and cheese is the perfect combination of flavors for a delicious, creamy dish. Loaded with bacon, creamy cheese and shallots, it is a delight for all cheese lovers.
Serving: 8
Preparation Time: 10 minutes
Ready Time: 45 minutes

Ingredients:
- 8 slices of bacon
- 2 shallots, minced
- 2 tablespoons of butter
- 2 cloves of garlic, minced
- 2 tablespoons of all-purpose flour
- 1 teaspoon of mustard powder
- 2½ cups of milk
- 2 cups of dry macaroni
- 2 cups of shredded sharp cheddar cheese
- 2 tablespoons of chopped fresh parsley
- Salt and pepper, to taste

Instructions:
1. Preheat oven to 375°F.
2. Heat a large skillet over medium heat. Cook bacon in the skillet until crisp, about 8 minutes; transfer bacon to a cutting board and let cool before chopping into small pieces. Set aside.
3. Add shallots to the skillet and cook until softened, about 5 minutes. Add butter and garlic and sauté until fragrant, about 2 minutes more. Stir in flour and mustard powder, and continue stirring for 1 minute. Slowly whisk in milk.

4. Bring milk mixture to a simmer and cook, stirring constantly, until slightly thickened, 4 to 5 minutes.

5. Cook macaroni according to package Instructions. Once cooked, drain and add to the sauce inside the skillet.

6. Stir in cheese, bacon, parsley and season with salt and pepper.

7. Transfer mac and cheese to a greased 9-inch baking dish and bake in pre-heated oven for 10 minutes, or until the top is golden brown.

Nutrition Information: Per serving (1/8 of the recipe): 305 calories, 13 g fat, 30 g carbohydrates, 18 g protein.

75. Shallot and mushroom quiche

Shallot and Mushroom Quiche
Serving - 8 slices
Preparation Time - 15 minutes
Ready Time - One hour

Ingredients:
4 eggs, 1/2 cup of half and half, 1/4 teaspoon of pepper, pinch of nutmeg, 1/2 teaspoon of salt, 9-inch deep-dish unbaked pie shell, 3 ounces of shallot, 4 ounces of fresh mushrooms, 2 tablespoons of butter.

Instructions: -
1. Preheat oven to 375 degrees F.

2. In a bowl, mix the eggs and half and half together. Add pepper, nutmeg and salt and mix well.

3. Melt the butter in a skillet and add the mushrooms and shallot. Cook for 3-5 minutes, stirring frequently, until shallot and mushrooms are tender.

4. Spread the shallot and mushroom mixture into an unbaked 9-inch deep-dish pie shell.

5. Pour egg mixture into the pie shell.

6. Bake at 375 degrees Fahrenheit for 40 minutes or until knife inserted in center comes out clean.

7. Cool for 5-10 minutes before cutting.

Nutrition Information - Calories: 165; Total Fat: 11 g; Saturated Fat: 5 g; Sodium: 295 mg; Carbohydrates: 11 g; Dietary Fiber: 1 g; Protein: 6 g; Cholesterol: 109 mg.

76. Shallot and Parmesan roasted potatoes

Shallot and Parmesan Roasted Potatoes
Serving: 4
Preparation Time: 10 minutes
Ready Time: 40 minutes

Ingredients:
- 4 large Russet potatoes, cut into 1-inch cubes
- 2 shallots, chopped
- 2 tablespoons olive oil
- 3 cloves garlic, minced
- 1/2 cup grated Parmesan cheese
- 2 teaspoons Italian seasoning
- Salt and freshly ground black pepper

Instructions:
1. Preheat oven to 400°F.
2. Place potato cubes on a baking sheet.
3. In a small bowl, mix together the shallots, olive oil, garlic, Parmesan cheese, Italian seasoning, and salt and pepper.
4. Gently toss the potato cubes in the mixture to coat evenly.
5. Place baking sheet in the preheated oven and bake for 30-40 minutes, or until potatoes are golden brown and tender.
6. Serve hot.

Nutrition Information:
Calories: 210 kcal, Carbohydrates: 27 g, Protein: 7 g, Fat: 8 g, Saturated Fat: 2 g, Cholesterol: 6 mg, Sodium: 360 mg, Potassium: 519 mg, Fiber: 2 g, Sugar: 1 g, Vitamin A: 135 IU, Vitamin C: 30.7 mg, Calcium: 112 mg, Iron: 2.2 mg

77. Shallot and goat cheese stuffed portobello mushrooms

Shallot and goat cheese stuffed portobello mushrooms
Serving: 4
Preparation Time: 15 minutes
Ready Time: 18 minutes

Ingredients:
- 4 large portobello mushroom caps
- 1/2 cup shredded mozzarella cheese
- 2 tablespoons olive oil
- 2 shallots, finely chopped
- 4 ounces soft goat cheese
- 2 tablespoons chopped fresh chives
- 1/4 teaspoon ground black pepper

Instructions:
1. Preheat the oven to 350 degrees F (175 degrees C). Grease a baking sheet.
2. Place the mushroom caps on the baking sheet.
3. In a medium bowl, mix together the mozzarella cheese, olive oil, shallots, goat cheese, chives, and pepper.
4. Spoon the cheese mixture into the mushroom caps.
5. Bake for 18 minutes in the preheated oven, or until the mushrooms are cooked through and the cheese has melted.

Nutrition Information:
1 Serving: Calories: 222 kcal, Carbohydrates: 6 g, Protein: 10 g, Fat: 17 g, Saturated Fat: 8 g, Cholesterol: 33 mg, Sodium: 191 mg, Potassium: 326 mg, Fiber: 1 g, Sugar: 2 g, Vitamin A: 375 IU, Vitamin C: 1.8 mg, Calcium: 135 mg, Iron: 0.8 mg

78. Shallot and garlic roasted octopus

This shallot and garlic roasted octopus recipe is quick and easy to make, and is sure to impress your dinner guests. The octopus is roasted in the oven and tastes delicious with the onion and garlic flavours!

Serving: Serves 4

Preparation time: 10 minutes
Ready time: 40 minutes

Ingredients:
- 2 shallots, finely chopped
- 2 cloves of garlic, minced
- 2 teaspoons of olive oil
- 1 pound of octopus, cleaned and cut into bite-sized pieces
- Salt and pepper
- 2 tablespoons of fresh parsley, chopped (optional)

Instructions:

1. Preheat the oven to 375F.
2. In a large bowl, combine the shallots, garlic, olive oil, octopus, salt and pepper. Mix until the octopus is evenly coated.
3. Transfer the octopus mixture to a baking dish.
4. Bake in the preheated oven for 30 minutes, or until the octopus is cooked through.
5. Optional: Sprinkle the parsley over the octopus before serving.

Nutrition Information (per serving):
- Calorie: 108 kcal
- Carbohydrate: 5.2 g
- Protein: 14.4 g
- Fat: 3.2 g
- Sat Fat: 0.4 g
- Fiber: 0.7 g
- Sugar: 0.8 g
- Sodium: 479 mg

79. Shallot and herb roasted venison loin

Shallot and herb roasted venison loin is a delicious entree composed of venison roast paired with aromatics like shallots, fresh herbs and white wine.

Serving: 4
Preparation Time: 15 minutes
Ready Time: 1 hour and 15 minutes

Ingredients:
- 2-3 pound venison loin
- 4 shallots, diced
- 2 tablespoons of fresh herbs (rosemary and thyme)
- 2 cloves of garlic, minced
- 1/4 cup of white wine
- 2 tablespoons of olive oil
- 2 tablespoons of butter
- Salt and pepper to taste

Instructions:
1. Preheat oven to 375 degrees F.
2. Season venison loin all over with salt and pepper.
3. In a small bowl mix together shallots, fresh herbs, garlic and white wine and set aside.
4. Heat olive oil and butter in a large pan over medium-high heat.
5. Sear venison loin on all sides until browned, about 2 minutes per side.
6. Add shallot mixture to the pan and cook for 1 minute.
7. Transfer venison loin and shallot mixture to an oven-safe dish.
8. Roast in preheated oven for 45 minutes to 1 hour, until internal temperature reaches 125-130 degrees F.
9. Remove from oven and let rest for 10 minutes before slicing.

Nutrition Information:
Calories: 350, Fat: 17g, Carbs: 3g, Protein: 37g

80. Shallot and bacon wrapped chicken thighs

Shallot and Bacon Wrapped Chicken Thighs are a delicious and flavorful dish that is sure to impress your guests. The crispy bacon and sweet shallot pair perfectly with the succulent chicken thighs making it a perfect meal to serve at any dinner occasion.
Serving: 4
Preparation Time: 10 minutes

Ready Time: 40 minutes

Ingredients:
- 8 bone-in chicken thighs
- 4 shallots, finely diced
- 12 slices of bacon
- 1 tablespoon olive oil
- Salt and pepper

Instructions:
1. Preheat oven to 375°F.
2. Place chicken thighs in a bowl with olive oil, salt, and pepper. Mix until chicken thighs are thoroughly coated.
3. Wrap one slice of bacon and one piece of shallot around each chicken thigh. Secure with a toothpick.
4. Place chicken thighs on a parchment-lined baking sheet and bake for 30 to 40 minutes, or until chicken is cooked through and bacon is crisp.

Nutrition Information:
Calories: 329, Fat: 22g, Carbohydrates: 4g, Protein: 29g, Sodium: 375mg, Cholesterol: 11mg.

81. Shallot and mushroom crostini

Shallot and Mushroom Crostini is an appetizer filled with flavorful and earthy mushrooms and caramelized shallots. This quick appetizer makes a delicious addition to any meal!
Serving: 4
Preparation Time: 10 minutes
Ready Time: 25 minutes

Ingredients:
- 10-12 thin slices of good quality baguette
- 2 tablespoons olive oil
- 2 tablespoons butter
- 3 cloves of garlic, finely chopped
- ½ large shallot, finely sliced
- 2 cups sliced mushrooms

- ¼ teaspoon salt
- Ground black pepper, to taste
- 2 tablespoons fresh parsley, chopped
- 2 tablespoons freshly grated Parmesan cheese

Instructions:
1. Preheat the oven to 375°F. Line a baking sheet with parchment paper.
2. Arrange the slices of baguette onto the baking sheet and brush with olive oil. Bake for 15 minutes, until lightly toasted. Remove from the oven and set aside.
3. Heat the butter in a large skillet over medium-high heat and add the garlic and shallot. Saute for about 3 minutes, until the shallot is softened and lightly caramelized.
4. Add the mushrooms to the skillet and season with salt and pepper. Saute until the mushrooms are tender and golden, about 10 minutes.
5. Remove the mixture from the heat and stir in the parsley and Parmesan cheese.
6. Top each crostini with a spoonful of the mushroom and shallot mixture.
7. Return the crostini to the oven and bake for an additional 5 minutes until the topping is lightly browned and crispy.
8. Serve hot.

Nutrition Information:
Calories: 137, Total Fat: 8g, Saturated Fat: 4g, Cholesterol: 13mg, Sodium: 342mg, Potassium: 101mg, Total Carbohydrates: 12g, Dietary Fiber: 1g, Sugar: 1g, Protein: 4g.

82. Shallot and herb roasted turkey legs

Shallot and Herb roasted turkey legs is a classic comfort food recipe - tender and juicy turkey legs cooked to perfection with a variety of onions, herbs and seasonings. This is a great dish for a special occasion or even a weeknight dinner.
Serving: 4
Preparation Time: 10 minutes
Ready Time: 1 hour

Ingredients:
- 4 turkey legs
- 2 shallots, finely chopped
- 2 tablespoons fresh thyme
- 2 teaspoons fresh rosemary, lightly chopped
- 2 tablespoons olive oil
- 1 teaspoon sea salt
- ½ teaspoon black pepper

Instructions:
1. Preheat oven to 375°F.
2. Place turkey legs in baking dish. Sprinkle shallots, thyme, rosemary, olive oil, sea salt and black pepper over the top.
3. Roast in preheated oven for 45 minutes, or until the turkey is cooked through and the internal temperature reaches 165°F.
4. Remove from oven and let rest for 10 minutes before serving.

Nutrition Information:
Calories: 450, Fat: 15g, Protein: 54g, Carbs: 4g, Fiber: 1g, Sodium: 350mg

83. Shallot and Parmesan roasted radishes

Shallot and Parmesan Roasted Radishes – an incredibly simple dish that packs a punch of flavor. This combination of roasted radishes, shallots, and Parmesan cheese is the epitome of comfort food that can be enjoyed all year long.
Serving: 4
Preparation Time: 10 mins
Ready Time: 40 mins

Ingredients:
- 8 radishes, trimmed and halved
- 2 shallots, thinly sliced
- 2 tablespoons olive oil
- Salt and pepper, to taste
- 2 tablespoons Parmesan cheese

Instructions:

1. Preheat the oven to 350°F (175°C).
2. Place the radishes and shallots on a sheet pan. Drizzle with olive oil and season with salt and pepper.
3. Roast in the oven for 25–30 minutes until the radishes are tender.
4. Sprinkle with Parmesan cheese and bake for an additional 5–7 minutes until cheese is melted and fragrant.
5. Serve warm and enjoy!

Nutrition Information (per serving):
Calories: 119, Total Fat: 8.3g, Sodium: 200mg, Carbohydrates: 9.7g, Fiber: 3.4g, Sugars: 3.3g, Protein: 4.6g.

84. Shallot and goat cheese stuffed squash blossoms

Shallot and goat cheese stuffed squash blossoms are an irresistible combination of savory flavors. Enjoy them as an appetizer or light meal, with a beautiful presentation.
Serving: Serves 4
Preparation Time: 15 minutes
Ready Time: 65 minutes

Ingredients:
- 8 large squash blossoms
- 2 shallots, diced
- 2 oz goat cheese
- 2 tablespoons olive oil
- 1/4 teaspoon dry thyme
- 1/4 teaspoon garlic powder
- Salt & pepper to taste

Instructions:
1. Preheat oven to 350°F.
2. In a small mixing bowl, combine diced shallots, goat cheese, olive oil, thyme, garlic powder, salt and pepper.
3. Gently open each squash blossom and stuff with 1 tablespoon of the shallot and cheese mixture.
4. Place blossoms onto a baking sheet lined with parchment paper.
5. Bake for 25-30 minutes, or until fills are lightly browned and crisp.

Nutrition Information: Per serving: 130 calories; 10.7g fat; 12g carbohydrates; 3.3g protein; 0.64mg iron; 30mg sodium.

85. Shallot and garlic roasted sea scallops

This delicious shallot and garlic roasted sea scallops recipe will make a great appetizer or dinner. The savory flavors of the shallots and garlic pair perfectly with the sweetness of the scallops and the result is a beautifully cooked dish.
Serving: 4
Preparation Time: 10 minutes
Ready Time: 30 minutes

Ingredients:
- 2 tablespoons of olive oil
- 2 tablespoons chopped fresh shallots
- 4 cloves of garlic
- 1 1/2 pound of large sea scallops
- Salt and pepper to taste

Instructions:
1. Preheat the oven to 375°F.
2. Heat the olive oil in a large oven-safe skillet over medium heat.
3. Add the shallots and garlic and cook for about 2 minutes.
4. Add the scallops and season with salt and pepper.
5. Cook the scallops for 2 minutes, until the edges begin to turn golden.
6. Transfer the skillet to the preheated oven and bake for 15 minutes.
7. Serve immediately.

Nutrition Information: Per Serving: 196 calories; 10.6 g fat; 8.8 g carbohydrates; 16.8 g protein; 88 mg cholesterol; 805 mg sodium.

86. Shallot and herb roasted quail legs

Shallot and herb roasted quail legs is an elegant and flavorful dish made with herbed shallot roasted quail legs. The sweetness of the shallot

combined with the aromatic herbs makes this dish truly unique and utterly delicious!
Serving: 4 servings
Preparation Time: 15 minutes
Ready Time: 45 minutes

Ingredients:
- 4 quail legs
- 4 shallots, peeled and minced
- 1 tablespoon olive oil
- 1 teaspoon fresh rosemary, chopped
- 1 teaspoon fresh thyme, chopped
- 1 teaspoon fresh basil, chopped
- 1/2 teaspoon garlic powder
- Salt and pepper, to taste

Instructions:
1. Preheat oven to 400 degrees F.
2. In a large bowl, combine the minced shallot, olive oil, rosemary, thyme, basil, garlic powder, salt and pepper.
3. Lay the quail legs in a single layer in a baking dish.
4. Cover the quail legs with the shallot and herb mixture.
5. Place the baking dish in the preheated oven and roast for 30-35 minutes or until the quail legs are cooked through and golden brown.

Nutrition Information:
Calories: 201, Total Fat: 12g, Saturated Fat: 3g, Cholesterol: 57mg, Sodium: 37mg, Total Carbohydrates: 5g, Protein: 14g

87. Shallot and bacon potato gratin

Shallot and Bacon Potato Gratin is an indulgent side dish made from layers of thinly sliced potatoes, shallots, and bacon, baked in a creamy cheese sauce and topped with a crunchy Parmesan cheese crust. It's the perfect accompaniment to any dinner.
Serving: 8
Preparation time: 20 minutes
Ready time: 1 hour

Ingredients:
- 4 large potatoes, thinly sliced
- 2 shallots, minced
- 8 slices bacon, cooked and chopped
- 2 cups heavy cream
- 1 cup grated Gruyère cheese
- 1/2 cup grated Parmesan cheese
- 1 tablespoon olive oil
- 2 cloves garlic, minced
- 1 teaspoon fresh thyme leaves
- Kosher salt and freshly ground black pepper, to taste

Instructions:
Preheat oven to 350 degrees F. Grease a 9-inch baking dish with olive oil.
Layer the potatoes, shallots, and bacon in the prepared dish.
In a medium bowl, whisk together the cream, Gruyère cheese, garlic, thyme, salt, and pepper. Pour the cream sauce over the potatoes, shallots, and bacon. Top with the Parmesan cheese.
Bake for 50-60 minutes or until the potatoes are tender when pierced with a knife.

Nutrition Information:
Calories: 496 kcal, Carbohydrates: 17 g, Protein: 11 g, Fat: 42 g, Saturated Fat: 22 g, Cholesterol: 106 mg, Sodium: 439 mg, Potassium: 517 mg, Fiber: 1 g, Sugar: 1 g, Vitamin A: 1125 IU, Vitamin C: 14.3 mg, Calcium: 245 mg, Iron: 0.9 mg.

88. Shallot and mushroom stuffed bell peppers

This dish of Shallot and Mushroom Stuffed Bell Peppers is a delicious and nutritious vegetarian meal! It features shallots, mushrooms, bell peppers, and a savory, tasty sauce. The bell peppers are roasted to perfection and stuffed with a filling that will make your mouth water.
Serving: 4
Preparation Time: 25 minutes
Ready Time: 35 minutes

Ingredients:
- 4 bell peppers
- 2 tablespoons olive oil
- 2 shallots, diced
- 4-5 mushrooms, diced
- 1 cup cooked quinoa
- 1 teaspoon garlic powder
- 2 tablespoons Parmesan cheese
- 1/4 cup vegetable or chicken broth
- 1/4 teaspoon dried oregano
- 1/4 teaspoon dried basil
- Salt and Pepper to taste

Instructions:
1. Preheat your oven to 375°F.
2. Cut the top off of each bell pepper and remove the seeds. Place on a baking sheet lined with parchment.
3. Heat the oil in a pan over medium heat. Add the shallots and mushrooms and sauté for 3-4 minutes until lightly browned.
4. Add the quinoa, garlic powder, Parmesan cheese, broth, oregano, basil, and salt and pepper to the pan and stir to combine.
5. Fill each bell pepper with the quinoa mixture.
6. Place in the oven and bake for 20 minutes.
7. Turn the oven to broil and cook for an additional 2-3 minutes, or until lightly browned.
8. Serve immediately or store in the refrigerator up to 3 days.

Nutrition Information:
Serving Size: 1 stuffed bell pepper
Calories: 231
Total Fat: 7 g
Saturated Fat: 2 g
Carbohydrates: 31 g
Protein: 7 g
Sugar: 11 g
Fiber: 6 g

Shallot and Parmesan Roasted Turnips is a delicious and simple side dish that packs flavor in few simple Ingredients.
Serving: 4
Preparation Time: 5 minutes
Ready Time: 25 minutes

Ingredients:
- 2 lbs Turnips, quartered
- 2-3 Tablespoons Olive Oil
- 2-3 Shallots, thinly sliced
- 1/4 cup Parmesan Cheese
- Salt and Pepper, to taste

Instructions:
1. Preheat oven to 375°F.
2. Arrange turnips on a baking sheet lined with parchment paper
3. Drizzle olive oil over the turnips and add the shallots
4. Sprinkle Parmesan cheese and season with salt and pepper
5. Bake for 25 minutes or until turnips are tender

Nutrition Information:
Calories: 102, Fat: 6.1g, Carbs: 10.4g, Protein: 2.6g

Shallot and goat cheese stuffed figs
Serving: 4
Preparation Time: 20 minutes
Ready Time: 40 minutes

Ingredients:
- 8 figs
- 1 shallot, diced
- 4 ounces soft goat cheese
- 2 tablespoons maple syrup
- 1 tablespoon balsamic vinegar

- 1 teaspoon fresh thyme

Instructions:
1. Preheat oven to 375°F.
2. Cut the tips off of the figs, making a small x-shape in the center.
3. In a small bowl, mix together the diced shallot, goat cheese, maple syrup, balsamic vinegar, and thyme until combined.
4. Stuff the figs with the combination cheese mixture.
5. Place the stuffed figs on a parchment-lined baking sheet.
6. Bake in preheated oven for 20 minutes.
7. Serve and enjoy!

Nutrition Information:
Calories: 114, Fat: 4g, Saturated Fat: 2g, Cholesterol: 9mg, Sodium:115mg, Carbohydrates: 16g, Fiber: 2g, Sugar: 11g, Protein: 4g.

91. Shallot and herb roasted duck legs

Shallot and Herb Roasted Duck Legs is a delicious and easy-to-make dish perfect for serving with a side of vegetables and mashed potatoes. This tender, juicy dish is bursting with flavor from the combination of herbs and shallots. Serve this tasty dish for a dinner guests or a special family meal.
Serving: 4
Preparation Time: 10 minutes
Ready Time: 1 hour

Ingredients:
- 4 duck legs
- 2 cloves garlic, minced
- 2 shallots, diced
- 2 tablespoons chopped fresh herbs (such as rosemary, sage, and/or thyme)
- 2 tablespoons olive oil
- Salt and black pepper, to taste

Instructions:
1. Preheat oven to 375°F (190°C).

2. Place the duck legs on a large baking sheet lined with parchment paper.
3. In a small bowl, combine the garlic, shallots, herbs, olive oil, salt, and pepper.
4. Rub the herb mixture on the duck legs.
5. Bake for 45 minutes to an hour, until the duck is golden brown and crispy.
6. Serve with vegetables and mashed potatoes.

Nutrition Information (per serving): Calories 350, Fat 21g, Cholesterol 97mg, Sodium 160mg, Carbohydrates 12g, Protein 25g.

92. Shallot and garlic roasted mussels

Shallot and garlic roasted mussels is a delicious and savory dish that is great for sharing with friends and family. It is easy to prepare and packed full of flavor.
Serving: 4
Preparation Time: 10 minutes
Ready In: 25 minutes

Ingredients:
• 2 tablespoons olive oil
• 1/2 cup diced shallots
• 2 cloves of garlic, chopped
• 2 pounds mussels
• 1 tablespoon butter
• 1/2 cup white wine
• 2 tablespoons fresh parsley, minced
• Salt and pepper to taste

Instructions:
1. Preheat oven to 400 degrees F.
2. Heat 1 tablespoon of olive oil in a large skillet over medium heat.
3. Add shallots and garlic to the skillet and cook for 2 minutes, stirring until fragrant.
4. Add mussels to the skillet along with the remaining olive oil, butter, wine, parsley, salt and pepper. Stir to thoroughly combine.

5. Transfer the contents of the skillet to a baking dish.
6. Place the baking dish in the oven and roast the mussels for 15-20 minutes until the mussels are cooked and open.
7. Serve the roasted mussels hot.

Nutrition Information: Per serving: 270 calories; fat 13.4g; saturated fat 4.7g; cholesterol 75mg; sodium 513mg; protein 20.1g; carbohydrates 13.3g; fiber 2.1g; sugar 0.4g

93. Shallot and bacon wrapped dates

This tasty appetizer combines salty bacon with sweet, juicy dates and crunchy shallots to create an irresistible snack.
Serving: Makes 12 Servings
Preparation Time: 15 minutes
Ready Time: 20 minutes

Ingredients:
- 12 pitted dates
- 12 shallot slices
- 12 bacon slices

Instructions:
1. Preheat oven to 375°F.
2. Wrap each date in a slice of bacon and shallot.
3. Place bacon-wrapped dates on a baking sheet.
4. Bake for 15 minutes, or until bacon is cooked through.

Nutrition Information (per serving): 170 calories; 9.1g fat; 14.5g carbohydrates; 3.3g protein.

94. Shallot and mushroom stuffed zucchini boats

Shallot and mushroom stuffed zucchini boats are a delicious vegan dinner that can be made in no time. This meal is satisfying even for the pickiest of eaters and is packed with flavor and nutrition.
Serving: 4

Preparation Time: 10 minutes
Ready Time: 30 minutes

Ingredients:
- 3 zucchinis
- 2 tablespoons extra-virgin olive oil
- 2 shallots, chopped
- 8 ounces mushrooms, diced
- 3 garlic cloves, minced
- 2 sprigs of fresh thyme
- 2 tablespoons fresh parsley, chopped
- 1/4 teaspoon sea salt
- 1/4 teaspoon freshly ground black pepper
- 1/2 cup gluten-free breadcrumbs

Instructions:
1. Preheat oven to 350°F.
2. Cut each zucchini in half lengthwise. Using a spoon, scoop out the insides, creating a boat shape.
3. Heat oil in a large skillet over medium-high heat. Add shallots and mushrooms and cook for 5 minutes or until mushrooms are tender.
4. Add garlic, thyme, parsley, salt, and pepper and cook for 1-2 minutes more.
5. Transfer mixture to a bowl and stir in the breadcrumbs.
6. Stuff each zucchini boat with the mushroom mixture. Place zucchini boats on a lined baking sheet.
7. Bake for 20-25 minutes, or until the zucchinis are tender.

Nutrition Information:
Each serving contains 169 calories, 8g of fat, 19g of carbohydrates, 5g of protein, and 4g of fiber.

CONCLUSION

Shallot Sensations: 94 Delicious Recipes is a cookbook that aims to bring the humble yet versatile shallot to the forefront of every home cook's kitchen. The cookbook features a plethora of recipes that showcase the shallot's unique flavor and texture, from appetizers to entrees to desserts.

Throughout the cookbook, the author provides tips on how to properly prep and cook shallots, making it accessible to even the most novice of cooks. The recipes are organized by meal course and are easy to follow, with clear instructions and ingredient lists.

One of the standout features of this cookbook is its wide range of recipes - there is truly something for everyone. From classic French dishes like beef bourguignon and quiche lorraine to Asian-inspired fare like shallot fried rice and ramen, Shallot Sensations offers a global perspective on this versatile ingredient.

Another aspect of the cookbook worth noting is the author's creativity in incorporating shallots into unexpected dishes, like shallot ice cream and shallot jam. These unique recipes are not only delicious, but also demonstrate the ways in which shallots can be utilized in a variety of ways beyond their traditional uses.

One of the biggest strengths of this cookbook is its focus on seasonal and fresh ingredients. Many of the recipes feature vegetables and herbs that are in season, which provides a heightened level of flavor and nutrition. Additionally, the author emphasizes the importance of sourcing high-quality produce, meats, and dairy, which not only enhances the flavor of the dish but also supports local and sustainable farming practices.

Overall, Shallot Sensations: 94 Delicious Recipes is a cookbook that is both accessible and adventurous. The recipes provide a great starting point for home cooks looking to incorporate shallots into their dishes, while also offering unique, unexpected dishes for more experienced cooks. This cookbook is sure to inspire cooks of all skill levels to experiment with the flavorful and versatile shallot.

In conclusion, Shallot Sensations: 94 Delicious Recipes is nothing short of a masterpiece. Its focus on one key ingredient takes it to new heights, offering a wealth of information on how to use this versatile item. Its exquisite, detailed wording makes cooking with shallots an attainable, fun experience. The book's international flare provides a journey through a variety of different foods and flavors, each specially curated to highlight shallots in their own way. Ultimately, this cookbook can transform even the most mundane dish and turn it into something exquisite. Truly, Shallot Sensations: 94 Delicious Recipes is as much a cookbook as it is a culinary journey through the world of shallots.

Printed in Great Britain
by Amazon

53328565R00056